CROSSING THE SOUL'S RIVER

CROSSING THE SOUL'S RIVER

A RITE OF PASSAGE FOR MEN

WILLIAM O. ROBERTS JR.

THE PILGRIM PRESS   CLEVELAND, OHIO

The Pilgrim Press, Cleveland, Ohio 44115
© 1998 by William O. Roberts Jr.

Printed in the United States of America on acid–free paper

03   02   01   00   99   98   5   4   3   2   1

Library of Congress Cataloging–in–Publication Data
Roberts, William O., 1942–
    Crossing the soul's river : a rite of passage for men / William O.
Roberts.
        p.   cm.
    Includes bibliographical references.
    ISBN 0-8298-1259-8 (pbk. : alk. paper)
    1. Middle aged men—Religious life. 2. Midlife crisis—Religious
aspects—Christianity. 3. Initiation rites—Religious aspects—
Christianity. 4. Jungian psychology—Religious aspects—Christianity.
I. Title.
BV4579.5.R63   1998
248.8'42—dc21   98-10499
                                                          CIP

REMEMBERING

JON HIGGINS,

STU ELLIOTT,

AND MY BROTHER, KEN

CONTENTS

Life is about transitions. We are born. We die. In between we grow up, and, if we are lucky, we grow old. This book is about one of those transitions—the transition that men face at midlife. This transition is described in different ways. It has been called the *grand mal* of all of life's transitions—literally, "the big bad"; as such, it is a thing to be avoided. It has also been dismissed as nothing but a passing intimacy crisis; as such, it is a thing to be ridiculed.

Both of those characterizations miss its real significance. The midlife passage is not, at its core, about buying a new red sports car, or about a fling with some young thing, or even about changing careers or accepting the fact that you are growing older. Rather, it is about the transformation of consciousness that can be accomplished only by addressing what I call the four soul tasks: (1) the breakdown of the persona—the superficial identity one develops in the first half of life; (2) the encounter with the shadow—the dangerous side of the personality we have learned to avoid; (3) the encounter with the soul-mate—the contrasexual aspects of our personality; and (4) the dialogue with the self.

Yet this book is more than just a description of those four soul tasks. It tells of a rite of passage, which might help individual men to address the challenges of midlife in a more effective manner. But its greatest value will be realized when this rite of passage is used by groups of men. I have in mind men's groups in churches, synagogues, or mosques, but it could be adapted to fit a variety of situations, such as retreats for corporate executives or even gatherings of fraternal groups.

The book is constructed on a notion that in the middle of the confusing wilderness of midlife, there is a life–giving river, which we have called the soul's river. Its mere presence in the center of this part of our life invites us to cross it. Its promise is that if we are successful in that crossing, we will pass from early adulthood to later adulthood with renewed vision and vitality.

The first part of the book helps us find our way through the wilderness to the river. The book then introduces us to a way to ford the river, using a model that has been used by human societies for centuries—a rite of passage, that is, a set of myths and rituals that help us to navigate the passage and engage the soul tasks in a manner that is safer and more certain than if we attempt it on our own, without guidance or a guide. The second part of the book discusses each of the four soul tasks and describes that part of the rite of passage that helps us address the task and accomplish it successfully.

I have lived through a midlife passage that was very challenging, and, although I had excellent psychotherapeutic help, I had no supportive community and certainly nothing like a rite of passage that might have dignified my struggles. Furthermore, I have had the benefit of talking with men, individually and in groups, of differing cultures and ages, and have discovered that many of them battle with the same issues. Indeed, because of those conversations, I am now persuaded that the book is not only for men in classic midlife, but might be helpful to men in their twenties, not so much to help them avoid the trials of midlife as to understand them when they present themselves.

This book arises not only from my own experience and the men's needs that this uncovered. It also arises from a long–standing interest in writing and speaking on this subject. In the early 1960s I lived in the Gambia in West Africa and was introduced to classic rites of passage. In the early 1970s I created a rite of passage to adulthood for the adolescents of a Congregational church in Middletown, Connecticut. In the early 1980s I wrote a book about that experience, published by Pilgrim Press as *Initiation to Adulthood: An Ancient Rite of Passage in Contemporary Form.*[1]

Then, in the early 1990s, I received a call from a professor who intended to use my first book as the basis for a new book to be entitled *Celebrating Passages in the Church: Reflections and Resources.* It was to be a series of essays on each of life's major passages, including childhood, adolescence, marriage, divorce, retirement, and, most interestingly, both *male* midlife and *female* midlife. Without thinking, I volunteered to write the chapters on men at midlife. When I was told that a respected and widely published theologian, a specialist in adult moral development, was writing those, I felt a bit embarrassed to have suggested my name. But several months later this noted author abandoned the project and I was invited to fill in, and I accepted immediately.[2]

At that point in my life, I had not actually led a rite of passage for men at midlife. I had led a men's group for years. I had led conferences on male friendships. I had stayed close to several male friends as they anguished through midlife. And, most important, I had personally survived, just barely, many of the trials associated with midlife.

Nevertheless, I wrote my chapter and sent the manuscript to the professor who was to edit and publish the book. For years I never heard another word from him. It was as if I had mailed my manuscript to a black hole. I now believe that black hole was a gift, because since my first attempt to write about a rite of passage for men at midlife, I have actually created one and led it. And it is powerful.[3]

In the course of developing this book I received help from many people. But there is one person whose contribution stands head and shoulders above all others. I became aware of this person's significant role in this project when one of the oldest and wisest women in our church, a woman who is appropriately named Grace, came to me with a few pointed words of instruction. "You better dedicate that book to Melissa. She is the real hero of the story."

I had to be honest and tell her that, since I had dedicated my first book to Melissa, I had already decided to offer this one in memory of two friends who died in the middle of their lives and to my brother who died at age forty-eight. But I do want everyone who reads this book to know of this wisdom from Grace.

Melissa agreed to marry me when we were both twenty-four years old. As a young adult I was reasonably stable. And I remained stable through the rest of my twenties and all of my thirties. It was not until I passed the threshold of my fortieth birthday that my life became troubled. I can now see that Melissa was the one who got hit with the brunt of that troubled life. In retrospect, I realize that she did everything possible to stay with me during the terrible days and nights of my transition.

I am now in my late fifties. The turmoil of midlife has passed; indeed, I am so bold as to claim that my midlife transition has proven transformational. But in the course of writing this book and having it published, we inevitably return to that painful time of life. This hurts her deeply. So I thank her for staying with me, once again, for struggling with me in the writing and rewriting of the book—and in its being made public. It is my hope that, as our marriage has been tested and made stronger, the book might help others in their own relationships.

INTRODUCTION:
STILL LIVING THE SAME OLD LIFE?

It was Christmas week. Life felt more stable than it had in many years. I had left my work and my role as a minister two Christmases ago, and now I was surprisingly settled and satisfied in a new career. I had separated from my wife and children four years ago, and now I was part of the family again. The boys were home from college. We were at a video store looking for a movie that we could watch as a family when I spied one called *Middle Age Crazy.* When no one was looking, I rented it. When no one was home, I watched it.

The story is so familiar as to be hackneyed. It begins at a birth-day party—a fortieth birthday party for a man who has every-thing—a beautiful wife (played by Ann-Margret, then many a man's fantasy woman) who has just arrived at her sexual maturity and has multiple bingos every time they make love, a lucrative ca-reer as an architect, a gracious home, two healthy parents, a seem-ingly well-adjusted son, a fine complement of friends . . . and a nagging uneasiness that somehow there is something missing.

As the story unfolds, his father dies, his well-adjusted son cannot adjust to college and returns home with a pregnant girl-friend, his wife decides to play bingo with a young policeman, and his father dies. He is going through what is called his midlife cri-sis. The nagging uneasiness is brought to full bloom by a question from his sister as they drive to their father's funeral: "You still driv-ing this same old car?" He rightly hears, "You still living the same old life?" And within days he is at the new car dealer trying to buy a new life for himself:

~ He trades his old Oldsmobile for a sporty new Porsche.

~ He replaces his wing tips and business suits with cowboy boots and a metallic blue shirt.

~ He compromises his career by missing appointments with his biggest client and shucking his reputation for reliability and thoroughness.

~ He spies the girl of his dreams and pursues her to her bedroom.

About the woman: She is a Dallas Cowgirl cheerleader who just happens to be an interior decorator who would do anything to have a meaningful relationship with a successful architect who can help her with her career. (Her own life journey has little to do with intimacy or sex, which comes to her easily, even naturally. Instead, she is seeking an identity and hoping to make a name for herself.)

The story ends happily, but tragically. It's happy, I guess, in that by the closing scene he is "back to his old self," which means back in his hot tub with Ann-Margret. It's tragic in that the poor man has no idea what happened to him. He is simply embarrassed to have been middle-age crazy and glad he's "normal" again. He'll try to get through all the remaining years of his existence not thinking about this terrible stretch of his life. He's not more conscious. He's not more aware. He's not more complex or interesting. He's certainly not more whole.

Most men do not experience such a dramatic midlife crisis. But every man faces the need to become more conscious, more aware, more complex—that is, to cross the soul's river.

This I have learned the hard way. Indeed, I was middle-age crazy, pretty much like that poor guy in the movie. But, if I may be so presumptuous, I believe that I learned from the experience. It's as if my craziness led me to a new level of sanity, as if my breakdown contributed to a breakthrough. These insights—and the ritual that men can share to make the crossing more communal and less arduous—will prove helpful for men who begin this work earlier, attend to it more often, and cross the soul's river throughout their lives.

Thus I tell my story—with great trepidation. My fears are at least three. First, I am concerned that someone will read about my crazy period and judge me in unkind ways. Second, I know that the telling of my tale inevitably touches bruises that are still tender. And third, I am deeply concerned that my story will overwhelm the main idea of this book, namely, that the male midlife passage is an incredible opportunity for growth that needs a rite of passage to support it. Nevertheless, I will take the risk of sharing some of what I experienced.

Yet, I will not get stuck in my own story. I have had the unusual opportunity to be with men in the midst of their midlife craziness. They have told their stories to me and allowed me to share at least portions of their stories, which I do with gratitude.

But more important even than that, through a rather strange set of circumstances, I have actually created and led a rite of passage for men at midlife. I have seen how men who have the rare opportunity to find themselves in a safe and caring community of brothers, and who share both myths and rituals that dramatize and potentialize the classic issues of midlife, can benefit deeply.

Let me tell you about some of those benefits. These men do not feel so alone. They do not feel so crazy. They are, generally speaking, less likely to react to the presenting symptoms of midlife craziness and more willing to stay with those issues until they discover their deeper significance for their lives. This means, in many cases, they do not find it necessary to abandon the lives they have created—their wives, their children, their livelihood, or their early callings. Rather, they are able to use this increased consciousness to move into the second half of life as more soul-centered human beings.

To say it another way—through the rite of passage for men at midlife, they come to realize that the issues are not essentially exterior to them, but interior. And in the safety of mystery rites and the community that the rite provides, they develop the confidence and the skills for the journey to their interiors, where they find themselves transformed.

The rite of passage for men at midlife, then, provides a map through the wilderness that has running through its center the "soul's river." The map is more like a topographical map than a road map. It shows men how to approach the river and then what they need to know to ford it. The map points out the depths and the shallows—where the wading is treacherous and the currents are strong, where men are likely to be in over their heads as they experience intense growing pains. It also indicates where the way is easy, sometimes almost so easy that if they are not careful men will slip on those slippery rocks and fall in. The rite even shows what the ground looks like on the other side, the mountain peaks men can climb after they have traversed the river, peaks from which they can get a much better look at the vistas that stretch out through the next stages of their lives—as well as glimpses into their deaths—and beyond.

I wrote this book because I had to. I won't tell you my whole story, of course, but the simple fact is that I have survived a midlife passage with the help of excellent psychotherapy, but without the support of a community or anything like a rite of passage. In my mid-forties, after years of turmoil, I left the life I had created and began my lonely wandering. I am now back with my life, and that life is remarkably lively, much more so than it possibly could have been if I had not suffered through midlife.

To be more specific, for twenty-five years I had one life as an academician (assistant dean of admissions and lecturer in religion at Wesleyan University) and a clergyman (a Presbyterian minister in Las Vegas and a Congregational minister in Middletown, Connecticut). I was also a husband, the father of three sons, and a respected citizen in Middletown. Then I left all of that and became unemployed and separated from my wife and family.

After several months I managed to get a job in a different culture. I was hired as a senior consultant with KPMG Peat Marwick, one of the (then) Big Eight accounting firms. My job was to help large corporations manage traumatic change caused by mergers, buyouts, reorganizations, and all the rest. I was to guide individuals caught up in those changes, helping them manage both themselves and others in a humane way.

While I was in the midst of an assignment with Merrill Lynch Realty, that national real estate firm was purchased by Prudential. The new owners offered me a position as senior vice president of Prudential Residential Services working primarily in New York and New Jersey and secondarily in Connecticut and Massachusetts. So within a year of the time I had been a minister of an urban church, I was a vice president with a major corporation.

In May 1993, I left the satisfactions and securities of that salaried position and began my own consulting practice, dealing with such issues as managing change, women and men working together, and career and life transitions. My practice is quite successful. In the last few years my clients have included several Fortune 500 companies.

Yet some of the most exciting assignments involve smaller organizations—boards of directors of charitable foundations grappling with conflict, planning committees of towns and cities searching for a vision, a law firm wondering why women and minorities don't get to be partners, a symphony orchestra struggling to stay viable in these tough times, and groups of primary-care physicians trying to cope with the traumatic changes in the health care industry. I continue to counsel individuals in career transitions.

In this new role as consultant, I strive to bring many of the concerns of my ministry to my work with my clients. I find remarkable receptivity to my ideas and even to my language. People are concerned about the soul—even in corporate America.[1]

Still more amazing to me, I find that my clients have much to teach me. Most of those who contract for my services consider themselves to be hard-nosed businesspeople who are eminently practical, so when we find ourselves considering issues such as changing a corporate culture, establishing new patterns of communication, or rethinking how work can be organized, these people do not get hung up on theories or ideologies. They ask, "Will this work?" Often the only way to know is simply to do it. They are prepared to learn from the actual experience. Time and again, in the experience itself, if I can stay responsive to the wisdom of the group, I discover that those old values I cultivated in the church are being sought in the business world.

One of the most dramatic examples of this occurred early in my new role. One December a partner and I were working with a Vermont bank that was rightsizing (or "downsizing" or "reengineering"). In place of traditional outplacement services, the bank had contracted with us to lead our week-long career transition workshop. As the group began to coalesce, I found myself slipping and referring to the bank as the "church." I was embarrassed at my mistake because it seemed so unprofessional.

But at one point, when the participants were wondering about their sadness as Christmas approached, I gave myself permission to use some of my understandings of a phenomenon frequently labeled "holiday blues" or "Christmas depression," a common and confusing melancholy that many people know at many holidays and anniversaries.

At Christmastime, every mall, radio station, and elevator seems to play carols. And they are relentlessly happy: "God rest ye merry, gentlemen/Let nothing you dismay"; "Good Christian friends rejoice"; "Joy to the world." For years I have felt that the psyche unwittingly strives to balance all this glee and becomes somber. "It would be better," I told the group, "to sing the one Christmas carol that expresses our ambivalence—'O Little Town of Bethlehem . . . the hopes and fears of all the years are met in thee tonight.'"

That single sentence freed the group to engage their career transitions much more fully. Singing about both hopes and fears in the same breath, they were able to start thinking more fully about the uncertainties of the future. On the one evening when we invited spouses or children or friends to come to a meeting, the participants asked me to explain the choice of "O Little Town of Bethlehem" as their way of asking permission to feel deeply the ambivalence of the change they were undergoing.

From that point on, we noticed that several members of the group began to make the same slip that I had been making—they referred to the bank as the church. One participant, a non–church-goer, indeed a non–Christian, thanked us for doing this. "This group is exactly what I would be looking for in a church," he said. "In fact, this is the first time I have ever approached Christmas actually feeling religious." From that day on, I have been willing to share my faith no matter how secular the setting.

I feel very fortunate. My professional life seems to be realigned with my deepest values. My work is profoundly satisfying. And, even though sometimes it seems too good to be true, my marriage is also healthy. I am still married to my first wife. We separated for a long time. Then we moved to the next step; the sheriff served divorce papers, and we hired lawyers. But we have been reconciled and our relationship is much more satisfying, certainly to me, than it had been for a long time. Our three sons are now fine young men.

Two final comments conclude this prologue—one about my writing style and another for any women who might be reading this book. First, my style includes some repetition—more than my editors would prefer. This sense of *déjà vu* is intentional. In my own learning and, therefore, in almost all of my teaching and training, I use what I have come to call the ratchet theory of learning. You probably know how a ratchet screwdriver works. The handle is turned, repeating the same motion time and again. In fact, to someone standing to the side, watching, the screwdriver's handle seems to be doing the same thing over and over. What the observer cannot see is that within the screwdriver is a mechanism that converts this repetitive action into a tightening (or loosening) action so that the screw itself keeps turning round and round, sinking ever deeper into the wood.

I kept that image of the ratchet screwdriver in mind as I wrote this book. We will go though the same motions again and again, but each time we do, we will introduce some new way of thinking about men at midlife and creating rites of passage for men at midlife. We will deepen our understanding using different language systems. We will begin with issues of adult development, then consider ideas from the new physics, then concepts from Jungian psychology, then personal stories or insights found in novels, then poetry. In fact, some of the same lines of poetry will be repeated.

The hope is that, as we repeat ourselves, we will probe more fully into the issues, until we arrive at our end, both the conclusion of this book and the purpose of this book. By then we will be able to stand with that legendary figure whose name was Job and realize what it means to dialogue with the voice that speaks from the whirlwind. We will be ready for the other side of the river, the next stage of life.

The second encouragement is for women readers. You are welcome not only to learn about what the men you know are facing but also to garner insights for yourself. It is only by accident that this book seems so masculine. When I was asked to do the original work on this topic, someone else was writing about women at midlife. Therefore, my initial focus was on the male sex.

And the male stuff can get thick. My examples come from men. All the legendary soul brothers who accompany us on our passage are men. The rites of passage that I have led have been for men only. Even my pronouns are often the old-fashioned masculine ones (again, to the chagrin of my editors).

But the perspectives of women have been important to me. As you will see throughout this book, it is often women who have taught me the next step in my male journey. I do believe that to a great extent women bring insights that men simply miss. Even more, I believe that so much of the moist, juicy, creative, daring living and loving that every human being craves is more difficult for men. So I thank you women on behalf of myself and my brothers.

I also hope that you might benefit from the insights of this book not only in understanding your husbands or partners or colleagues at work but also in realizing that although the feminist movement has brought benefits to both sexes, it may also create for some of you the same pressures that have shaped and misshaped men for generations.

PART ONE

GAUGING THE SOUL'S RIVER

1

TESTING THE DEPTH

Recently, I received a letter from a corporate executive who had been in one of my training classes on sexual harassment. This particular class was held in California. We had spent the morning reviewing the evolving law on sexual harassment and doing exercises to help the participants see the deeper issues in gender communication and miscommunication. When we took a break for lunch, this man sought me out to tell me he was having some trouble with all of this.

I soon realized, however, that he was having trouble not with the training, but with his life. He was in the midst of an intimacy crisis and was in great personal pain. Although I rarely do this, I went to my briefcase and gave him a copy of an earlier generation of this book. He read it on the plane going home and wrote me immediately:

> I read your material. It was very upsetting. It cut so close to home. It was as if you knew everything about me. I became so agitated, in fact, that the woman next to me asked me if I was o.k. "You bet," I said; "for the first time in years I realize I am o.k. I just read about me in this paper and I now know I'm not crazy."

This man had responded to the fact that someone seemed to know his story, a story that he lived with a frightful intensity but shared with no one. Too confused and embarrassed and terrified to think anyone could possibly understand, he kept the smile on his face and the swagger in his voice and the pain of his existence deep inside him until he arrived at home. He shared what he called his truth with only one person—his woman.

GENDER CONDITIONING FOR MIDLIFERS

To be honest, I was not surprised that he responded with such ve-hemence, because he had unwittingly played a major role in the drama I had created in the midst of that late-morning exercise on gender conditioning. When I was contracted by this Fortune 200 company to provide mandated training for all supervisors on han-dling sexual harassment, I knew that the training could not be de-livered in its traditional form—a two-hour session about the changes in the law that scares the daylights out of the participants. This problem should be addressed only in the broader context of the relationship between the sexes. To achieve this, I have created a simple exercise to make women and men conscious of the dis-tinctive gender conditioning. Such an exercise can begin by asking participants to visualize an earlier time of life:

> Please take a moment and transport yourself back to your adolescence, somewhere between thirteen and sixteen years old. Picture yourself in your high school and think about what you heard about being a man and a woman. More specifically, identify the boys who were becoming real men. Who were they? What did they do? What did they look like? How could you tell they were going to be-come real men?
>
> When you have finished that, identify the girls who were becoming real women. Who were they? What did they do? What did they look like? How could you tell they were going to become real women?

When the instructions are complete, an awkward silence usually follows. Then one person starts to write. Then another. And finally most of the others. One can almost feel old memories come flooding into the room: dreams, hopes, fantasies, hurts, disappointments. Remembrances of old inadequacies. When this private process has finished, the participants are moved to the next stage. Reunion groups of five to ten persons are formed according to their high-school graduating classes. The members of each group are then asked to talk with one another about their high school. Soon the room is abuzz with those old memories. Full-grown adults have regressed to that troubled, transitional state called adolescence and are discovering that there are others who grew up in the same culture.

When the talk has built to a crescendo, as it usually does, I interrupt to get reports from the clusters to the full group. Who were the boys who were becoming "real men"? What did they do? What did they look like? Soon key words are voiced by each of the groups and quickly recorded: leaders, jocks, tall, muscular, drove fast cars, athletic, successful, drank, good athletes, winners, powerful. And who were the girls who were becoming real women? What did they do? What did they look like? Again, key words describing "real women" are shouted out and written down: pretty, caring, physically developed, big breasts, wore tight sweaters, sensitive, popular.

After the lists are long enough, a crystallizing question is raised. What actual boy are you remembering? What role did he play in the high school? "Captain of the football team" is the usual response. And who was the girl? "Captain of the cheerleaders" is the typical reply. These responses are challenged to check the accuracy of the perceptions.

You say the boy who was becoming a "real man" was the captain of the football team. But could it have been someone else, maybe the captain of the soccer or tennis or swimming team? Objections are shouted out. "You're crazy, Bill. It's the captain of the football team." What about a state champion miler? I ask. Or a guy who went to state band? "No!" They are almost indignant, "The captain of the football team!"

I grant the accuracy, but then ask, What about the girl who was becoming a "real woman"? Couldn't she be the valedictorian? "Get outta here," they usually retort. "She's the captain of the cheerleaders." How about the prom queen or the homecoming queen? "Of course, she's the same person as the captain of the cheerleaders!"

I have done this exercise maybe as many as a hundred times, and only once did I get a different answer. I tried the exercise on seventh graders and their parents. The parents came through true to form, but the students had no form. In many ways the next generation of young people has a different set of issues in establishing a sexual identity. Their options are greater, especially for the girls, but their confusion is also greater.

But there was no confusion for the parents, as there is no confusion for most of us now in the middle of our lives. When we were young, we knew that real men were captains of football teams and real women were captains of the cheerleaders. But was it also clear what these two figures did for our high schools and for themselves? So I ask that question next and get amazingly consistent answers. The captain of the football team did what? Got glory, built a reputation, made a name for the school, became famous, organized men to win, scored! Won! And the captain of the cheerleaders did what? Looked good, kept up the spirit, was enthusiastic, cheered when we won, encouraged us when we were behind, dated the captain of the football team, talked on the phone, got scored upon!

Even though the exact words vary from one group to another, the responses achieve the same central message. Real men perform; if they perform well, they score; if they score enough, they win; if they win enough, they make a name for themselves. That is how they become a success. Real women cheer on the team. They care, feel, keep up the spirit, look good (no, they look great). They also look for a partner.

On most occasions, when leading this exercise, I will turn to the group to find out how many men really were their high-school football captains and how many women actually led the cheerleaders. Generally, none of those are present. Then, our conversation turns to those of us who did not quite measure up to this image. We discuss the inadequacies we felt as adolescents, the ways that our gender cultures—the masculine and feminine cultures—led us to see ourselves as misshapen in some fundamental way. Often participants will recall and share particularly painful moments when they—we all—were dented by words or actions from someone representing the culture of the opposite gender.

In some groups, especially groups of senior corporate executives or salespersons, a few men will have been football captains. They are generally tall, distinguished looking, and carry a certain air of authority. Similarly, on occasion a former captain of the cheerleaders is present. She is most often younger than her male counterpart, shorter, attractive, and vivacious.

The executive who had taken the manuscript as he flew home from the workshop was once a football captain. In that particular group, a woman had once led the cheerleaders in her high school. So in that workshop I could interview the two of them about growing up male and female in America. At one point, when he was talking about how tough he used to be, I asked him what happened when he lost a game. Without missing a beat, he pointed to the cheerleader and said, "She cried."

When I heard that, I was stunned by the incredible truth he had just spoken. When the football star was hurting, the cheerleader expressed his pain. It was probably also true that when *he* felt great joy, *she* would have expressed those feelings as well. My hunch that this man still had a serious problem expressing feelings proved correct. Such a problem meant that he was ripe for an *intimacy crisis*, the most common but most superficial form of the midlife crisis.

ERIK ERIKSON'S EIGHT STAGES

When the group heard his response to my question of how he dealt with defeat, they suddenly knew in dramatic ways that more than the misuse of power is involved in the transaction of sexual harassment between women and men. More is at play in the conversation between the sexes than simple miscommunication. They were eager to learn more about how this happened. So we turned to a brief presentation on how women and men are conditioned by different cultures, and therefore, how we develop through different channels in adulthood.

In 1950, Erik Erikson wrote *Childhood and Society,* which lays out eight sequential psychosocial tasks. The first four psychosocial tasks occur in infancy or childhood. The second four begin in adolescence.

Trust is knowing that you are safe, that your parent (for those of us in midlife, it was usually our mother) will be there for you, even if at the moment she is out of sight. You come to trust your world to take care of you.

Autonomy is standing on your own two feet. *No* is the key word that marks transition into this stage. Which parent has to advise a two–year–old child, "Honey, you are now ready for your next psychosocial task. It would be appropriate for you to start saying no"? Children simply know that they need autonomy at about that age. So they just know that the word no will help them get it. It's as if "no" is embedded in the psyche, just waiting to come out at the right moment.

Initiative is the stage that is energized by the word *why*.

Industry is that condition on which elementary–school teachers count. It's part of the reason why teaching second, third, or fourth grade can be so gratifying. The students just want to learn; they are industrious.

When humans pass out of childhood, they enter a turbulent stage of life known as adolescence. Erikson tells us that the psychosocial task of adolescence is establishing an identity, which he describes this way: "*Identity* is a unity of personality now felt by the individual and recognized by others as having a consistency in time, a sense of inner self–sameness and continuity."[1] And in another context, "The sense of ego identity is the accrued confidence that the inner sameness and continuity prepared in the past are matched by the sameness and continuity of one's meaning for others, as evidenced by the tangible promise of a career."[2]

The individual and the society negotiate identity. The individual, by words and actions, proclaims, "This is who I am." Others react to the proclamation, affirming some of it and denying other parts of it. In response, the identity is modified, sometimes adjusting to the evaluation of others, at other times insisting on the original proclamation, and still at other times attempting something altogether new. At a certain point this back–and–forth process settles down, and the individual feels a certain resonance between who he sees himself to be and who society accepts him to be. If he is successful in establishing his identity, he will hear deep within himself society's affirmation, "Yes, that is who you are."

This is what a football captain does. All over this country, in town after town, on Friday night or Saturday afternoon, young men bang their heads against one another. The strongest and the quickest and the cleverest overpower the others or elude the others and *score*. If they score enough, they win. And when they win they get to gloat over their victory, while the fans in the stands, led by the loyal and devoted cheerleaders, proclaim their success. "We're number one! We're number one!" And then the next morning, those battered young heroes wake up, go to the front door, pick up the morning paper, and there, in bold print, are their names, both their individual names and the team name. And if they are really lucky, there in living color is their picture. Now they are somebody. Now they have an *identity*—felt by the individual and recognized by others.

When they have established an *identity*, according to Erikson, they are ready for *intimacy*:

> The young adult, emerging from the search for and the insistence on identity, is eager and willing to fuse his identity with that of others. He is ready for intimacy, that is, the capacity to commit himself to concrete affiliations and partnerships and to develop the ethical strength to abide such commitments, even though they may call for significant sacrifices and compromises. Body and ego must now be masters of the organ modes and of the nuclear conflicts.[3]

Erikson's paradigmatic case of intimacy is what he calls *true genitality*. "In order to be of lasting social significance, the utopia of genitality should include these three ingredients: (1) mutuality of orgasm (2) with a loved partner (3) of the opposite sex."[4]

My notion of intimacy is quite different from Erikson's and comes from the word's etymology. The Latin word *intimatus* means "inmost" or "innermost," as in "the innermost secrets of my heart." I do not believe that intimacy requires genitality; indeed, such a narrow perspective frightens us away from intimacies. We do not want genital involvement with members of our own sex, or even necessarily with members of the other sex. But we do want to know and to be known at the level of our innermost secrets.

In Erikson's scheme of things, only when one has established an appropriate identity and intimacy is she or he ready for the next stages—generativity and ego integrity. To Erikson, generativity "is primarily the concern in establishing and guiding the next generation. . . . The concept of generativity is meant to include such more popular synonyms as productivity or creativity, which, however, cannot replace it." The final developmental stage, ego integrity, is defined as "the ego's accrued assurance of its proclivity for order and meaning. It is the acceptance of one's one and only life cycle as something that had to be and that, by necessity, permitted no substitutions."[5]

Erikson views adult development as following a predictable course. Once the childhood psychosocial tasks are accomplished, we all move through the four remaining stages in this sequence—identity, intimacy, generativity, ego integrity. My own thinking about adult development differs from Erikson's in key ways. This difference has major implications for how women and men approach midlife and helps explain why the midlife passage is so much more turbulent for men than it is for women.

I came to this understanding when I was still a young man. In those years, when I was working intensely with adolescents to guide them through their perilous passage to adulthood, I frequently used Erikson's "Eight Stages." In fact I had his eight psychosocial tasks printed up on eight cards, which I would lay out on the ground or on the floor as I introduced these teenagers to the stretch of life from birth to death.

THE DISTINCTIVE PATTERNS OF WOMEN AND MEN

One winter weekend in the mid-1970s I took my cards of the Eight Stages to a retreat I was leading not for adolescents, but for adults. The retreat was on identity and intimacy. As I was making one presentation, laying out the cards, trying my best to give life an overview, one woman spoke up in words that initially felt like a challenge. "I think Erikson is wrong," she said. "I know he is wrong for me. And I'll bet he's wrong for a lot of women." I invited her to say more. "For me, and I think for most women," she continued, "intimacy comes before identity. When we're teenagers, intimacy is our concern. Identity is later, much later." And with that the room became alive with life stories. Women and men looking at life, our own lives, and wondering if there was some hidden logic to the ways in which women and men develop as adults.

Within the hour we had a different framework. Women, mostly, agreed with their sister. For them intimacy came before identity. The concern for identity came later, in most cases, much later. Men began to see life differently, too. "Identity isn't followed by intimacy. It's followed by generativity. In fact, as you are finishing off the task of establishing an identity, you are almost automatically drawn into the next task in finding a job, and a career. By the time you are a young adult you have got your calling—you're out to save the world."

Immediately the women saw the place of generativity differently, too. "That is also true for us. Intimacy leads to generativity.

Our children are means for us to make a contribution, to make a difference. Our jobs also. But children come to us, come from us, thank God, when we are young adults."

And with that we adapted Erikson and adopted a new framework for our lives. Twenty years after that weekend retreat when I first heard the wisdom of this particular group, I've never ceased to be amazed by it. As males and females, we pass though the *childhood* stages pretty much together. If we are cared for, then we will develop trust as infants. We both start saying no and becoming autonomous as terrible two–year–olds. We develop autonomy and industry as children.

For *Most* Men	For *Most* Women
Trust	Trust
Autonomy	Autonomy
Initiative	Initiative
Industry	Industry
IDENTITY	INTIMACY
GENERATIVITY	GENERATIVITY
INTIMACY	IDENTITY
Ego Integrity	Ego Integrity

Erikson's Stages of Development Adapted for Men and Women

But in *adolescence* our paths follow very different routes. Men seek an identity and then move to generativity. Women yearn for intimacy and then move to generativity. This means that in midlife, we come back to the other's adolescent task. Men yearn for intimacy. Women seek an identity.

Women in U.S. society seem to be making strides in gaining identities. I marvel at the strength of so many women of my generation in shifting from a derivative identity to an autonomous one. A *derivative identity* is one that comes from one's relationship with another. "I'm his wife" or sister or daughter or mother. In the workplace, a derivative identity says, "I'm so–and–so's secretary" or nurse or assistant or student. An *autonomous identity*, in contrast, establishes identity with less reference to relationships with others and says, "I am a distinctive person in my own right because of my own skills, my own competencies, my own drive, my own success."

Women are doing well in their quest, in part because of the strength of a great cultural force—the women's movement, which has helped both men and women. Furthermore, in many corporations, women get at least some encouragement from enlightened men within the power structure who realize that everyone benefits when talented persons, no matter what their sex, are included. Finally, many husbands support and even delight in their spouses' successes as they establish and develop their own skills.

For men, the situation is nearly the reverse. The male midlife quest is for intimacy. Men are neither graceful nor often successful in this quest. The men's movement, in both its secular (e.g., Robert Bly) and its evangelical (e.g., Promise Keepers) forms, remains a modest cultural force. Many men have given up trying to achieve intimacy with spouses who, after all, are more concerned with their own identity quest. And finally, at our jobs, even though it is in the work setting that we are most likely to find a person who can offer the intimacy we crave, we do not dare tell anyone what's going on deep inside us. Especially not with this overwhelming concern about sexual harassment.

But our situation is even more desperate. Our task is something we are not yet good at. We did not learn how to be sensitive and gentle and vulnerable in high school. We learned instead how to bang our heads and bodies into the opposing teams. In fact, we even learned how to organize other men to do likewise. We learned how to score, not how to know another person deeply or be known.

Before high school we never learned to respect and honor and express our feelings. When we hurt and cried we were told, "Grow up. Be a big boy. Big boys don't cry." When we were overjoyed about something and relished our success, we were told, "Get off your high horse. Settle down. Control yourself."

So we come to midlife with none of the natural skills that would prepare us for success in our quest, our yearning for intimacy. Should we be surprised that in our frustration, we work all the harder? Because as males we were taught never to give up, we try time and again when we fail. And in the trying we become obsessed with this yearning for closeness. And most often we screw up—badly.

The whole world notices our screwups. For example, if I say, "It's a midlife crisis," which sex comes to mind? Almost everyone answers "men." And if I say, "He's having a midlife crisis. What's happening?" Typical guesses from any group include having an affair, running off with his secretary, shacking up with his graduate student, cheating on his wife. However people put it, these screwups mean the same thing, namely, that men are making a mess in their quest for intimacy.

MAPPING THE MALE MIDLIFE

To see the male midlife crisis only as an intimacy crisis is to trivialize what can be an incredible opportunity for growth—indeed, a noble and necessary stage of growth. My passion about this comes from the self-ridicule and community ridicule I felt as I wandered alone through midlife. Voices of women grew louder as I overheard them say to their husbands and friends, "Be careful, or you'll become just like Bill." Voices of male friends grew fainter as they avoided me. My own voice demanded to know why I was such a fool, why I just did not pull up my socks and get back to where I belonged. But there was something inside me that simply could not do that. It was as if I had to remain in that wasteland of midlife until I knew what it meant. So I stayed there—alone and lost.

I wish someone had handed me a map of this strange land. To be honest, there was someone. But the map he gave me pointed out only the most obvious features. It identified the dilemma men at midlife face regarding their identity, but it did not go on to point out the more significant and challenging aspects of the passage. It did not take us far enough on the journey to see the rewards of our effort. Nevertheless, it made a valuable contribution.

Therefore we will begin to map out this terrain with Daniel Levinson's *Seasons of a Man's Life.* His book deals with the issue of identity by introducing the concept of the individual life structure, which gives us a framework for recognizing the engagements of the person with the society. "It requires us to consider both self and world and the relationships between them."[6] Each person's life structure can have various components—job, marriage and family, friendships, ethnic identities, religious commitments, hobbies, even fantasies and character traits. But the most central of all of these generally relate to our love and our work, that is, our families and our jobs.

As normal and healthy persons we live our lives, Levinson asserts, by developing a vacillating relationship to our life structures. There are times when we experience stability and times when we find ourselves in transition. In the stable periods, we resolve some fundamental issues and form our structure around those resolutions. Stable periods are times of consolidation. Transitional periods are times when questions present themselves with sufficient force to cause us to rethink some of our basic assumptions, and even to break up our individual life structures and move toward a new relationship with both self and society. Transitional periods are almost always times of confusion. They are also times of growth.

When I think about moving from stable periods through transitional periods and then back to new stable periods, I use an example from the natural sciences—the developmental stages of the lobster—to help clarify the process. It might seem as though the lobster is shaped by its shell, but actually it gives shape *to* its shell—to its individual life structure. That structure is marked by stages as it molts (loses its shell). During each stage, it makes its life conform to the size and shape of its structure. But as internal growth occurs, the lobster soon is restricted by this shell; it needs to break it in order to grow to its next stage of life. Between discarding the old shell and establishing its new shell—in this transitional time—the lobster wanders around in the ocean depths without the protective shell. It is now utterly vulnerable.

Levinson argues that these vulnerable, transitional times come at particular points in the life process. Gail Sheehy's bestseller *Passages: The Predictable Crises of Adult Life* is based on Levinson's work and underscores these transitional times as predictable. Both authors agree that we must break up our individual life structures, head out into the unknown, and create new individual life structures for ourselves. We, like the lobster, need to shed constraining structures and enter into a time of vulnerability.

Levinson charts this process with a simple diagram, his map of adulthood. In his map we begin adulthood in a box. At some point we break out of that box and enter a transitional time, dubbed by Levinson as the early adulthood transition. When we complete the transition we enter another box, where we stay for a long time. In due time we break out of that box, enter a second transitional stage, the middle adulthood transition, which leads to still another box. Eventually we break even this box, head out on our final transition, the late adulthood transition, which brings us to the box of old age.[7]

Later I will seek to revise Levinson's map, so that we do not go through life merely moving from one box to another. But at this point I want to focus our attention on the box of early adulthood, to see how it is formed, how it becomes solid, and how hard it is to break out of.

Young men, however, really work from the box (or shell) metaphor. They make a few key decisions and then begin to cluster energies around those decisions. For instance, the young man meets another person and thinks that he is falling in love. He asks questions of the other, such as, "Would you like to go out with me?" If the other says yes time and again, then the young man asks himself bigger questions: Is this the one? Should we get married? This can lead to developing a committed relationship, forming a home, contemplating a family, and so forth. Each time a young man has asked a question effectively, he has created more of an identity for himself. In the beginning it generally feels pretty good, even exciting. But sometime later, it can feel like a box or a confining shell.

This pattern applies to a young man's occupation and other aspects. Each time he asks a question, if an affirmative answer is given, then he takes the next step in constructing a box. If, however, he gets a negative answer, he has to re-create an identity, first in his own mind, and then socially until he gets an affirmation. Only then can he go on to create his box.

It is important to know that the box is, by definition, not infinite. It does have limits. There is, inevitably, a point at which the *I* stops and the *Not-I* begins. "I am a dentist, not an astronaut." "I am a good bread winner, not a lazy lout." "I am married to my wife and not free to pursue every fantasy that presents itself."

The early stages of this process are generally invigorating. But then, if he is *reasonably successful* and *reasonably creative*, he will often experience the box as confining. To be sure, if men are *not* reasonably successful, we will probably never build a distinctive enough identity that can box us in or seem restrictive. If we are *not* reasonably successful, we will be able to change all we want, and no one will notice.

Perhaps two extreme examples will help. A homeless man I know thinks he is a theologian and carries a copy of Paul Tillich's *Courage to Be* everywhere he goes. Whenever I see him, he wants to talk about Tillich's theology. I happen to like the man, and so I used to listen to him carefully, hoping to hear his wisdom. But as I listened, I discovered that he had never invested any of the hard work required to understand Tillich. So even though he deceives himself in thinking he has the identity of a theologian, he is not successful in establishing that identity. He could discard his book and get a new one, say a book about computers, and proclaim himself a computer expert. If he decides to make a major life change, it would not be much of a problem for him. No one will much notice or care.

But for my high-powered friend, who is an executive vice president of a bank, the situation is the reverse. He is the loving father of three children, the devoted husband of a lovely wife, and a well-respected member of the community. Should he try to change his identity—move out of his box—on some midlife journey, he will have a rough time. His very success in establishing his current identity keeps him from moving to other identities.

A reasonable level of success is a precondition for the midlife journey. So is a reasonable level of creativity. Some men do not seem to be curious about their lives. They do not question their current box; they do not quest for something else; they do not challenge the limits. This is not a matter of intelligence so much as psychological style. Some men are content, or at least sufficiently content, not to risk upsetting the status quo.

Perhaps at one time, a book such as this one would be written for the reasonably successful and creative man only. But I have been with too many men whose individual life structures were shaken by external events such as a corporate restructuring, the lab results from a biopsy, or the news that a loved one is in critical condition. In these circumstances, men are jarred into becoming creative with their lives.

This invitation to develop a more creative approach during midlife makes sense especially if one thinks of life from its beginning to its midpoint. When we are born, we are like a circle—we have potential. We can turn in any direction and develop ourselves. But in order to become someone distinctive, to achieve a particular identity, we make decisions with the help of parents and friends and teachers and siblings and, eventually, all of society. These decisions help us define ourselves. If one is resolved to be an accountant and a partner in the firm by the age of thirty-three, then one needs to focus on that goal, working hard, putting in many hours, and making significant sacrifices in order to fulfill that goal. Rather than developing yourself by enlarging the circle, you develop yourself by selecting a certain arc of the circle and focusing your attention there. This means that other aspects of one's potential are laid aside or ignored—until sometime later.

The world of work provides one major outlet for men. The world of love usually provides another. We are born with feeling for the whole world and all of its creatures. It's like this vast erotic connection. Then you start to focus your attentions by directing them toward one special person. You love that person, and perhaps form a committed covenantal relationship. At some point that love may branch out to include children. And in early adulthood, you relish the intensity of all that feeling for someone, formed in part by cutting off powerful feelings for others. Until later—which almost always comes. Then we want more out of the box. We do not want to limit life to the little piece of the pie we have carved out for ourselves. Indeed, we want out of the box. We want to smash our shell.

TRANSITION MORE THAN CRISIS

At that moment we are on the brink of a midlife crisis. Frankly, I prefer not to use the word *crisis* to describe what happens to men at midlife. It seems to conjure up images of panic, of being out of control. I prefer words like midlife *passage*, midlife *transition*, or even midlife *transformation*. But *midlife crisis* is the phrase our culture uses. So I am going to try to redeem the word, make it more than just an embarrassing put-down.

In my consulting work I get to be with persons who do not speak English as their first language. Often, they can help us understand meanings that are lost to us in the very words we use.

Two Greeks told me that the word *crisis* comes from the Greek word *krisis* (pronounced KREE–sus), which means "a stage in a sequence of events at which the trend of all future events, especially for better or worse, will be determined." Another definition is "a time of decision, when the future is determined for good or ill." *Krisis*, then, is a time of decision.

A man from France explained that the word *decision* comes from the French word *decider*, which means "to lose, to cut off, to fall off." A deciduous tree is one that loses its leaves so that new vitality can come into that living organism. When we make decisions, we experience loss.

The Chinese have taught the most. Their word for *crisis* is shown here. To the Chinese, *crisis* is comprised of two characters— *Wei* (on the right) and *Ji* (on the left). *Wei*, if taken alone, would mean danger. *Ji*, if taken alone, would mean opportunity. So *crisis* is a time of both danger and opportunity. When I was working in Hong Kong, participants in our training explained an additional element of mystery. "Chinese," they said, "is an ancient language, much older than English or, for that matter, any of the major European languages. Chinese words are actually little stories. The word for *crisis* is the story of a person taking a trip down a river. *Wei* refers to the rocks that are hidden beneath the surface. The most important dangers in any crisis are hidden dangers. *Ji* is the character for opportunity, but real opportunity is usually hidden in the mist, the mystery. You have to navigate around all those hidden dangers to get to the hidden opportunities." Then they explained the true challenge of hidden dangers. "Since you can't see them, you have to study the currents in the river. The river knows how to steer you through the crisis, if you can learn to trust it." (Hence, this book's title is *Crossing the Soul's River.*)

When we begin to apply this ancient wisdom to the midlife crisis, we realize that most of us do not know how to derive the benefits from this deep ambivalence that is summed up in the words *Wei* and *Ji*—danger and opportunity. We know a lot about the *dangers* of midlife. We know much less about the *opportunities*, because so few of us persevere on the journey far enough to get to the place where the hidden opportunities reveal themselves. Most men encounter the dangers and rush back into the box,

Chinese Word for *Crisis*

maybe having learned a little, but missing most of the mysterious opportunities for profound change.

In most cases we do not even know how the opportunities might present themselves. There is an old saying, "Opportunity knocks only once." I believe opportunity is more generous. It will knock time and again, but without some encouraging response, opportunity will just go on its way. How does opportunity come knocking at midlife? Sometimes one hears it tapping from the outside, from events exterior to and beyond one's control—the death of a child or sibling or parent, divorce, job termination or career collapse. Or perhaps, less dramatic but equally perplexing changes are opportunity's signals—a child leaves home, one's spouse strikes out on a new career quest and search for identity, or one's hair or physical stamina becomes depleted. Or perhaps the strange call to midlife opportunity starts knocking deep within—unexplained moodiness, sleeplessness, lethargy, anxiety, fear of death.

Often the knocking takes the form of depression. Our culture has an uneasy relationship with depression. On the one hand, we are encouraged to live the happily–ever–after mentality first taught in childhood fairy tales. We are shielded from a whole body of fairy tales about men and women at midlife.[8] These tales address issues of maturity over many years and do not deceive us into thinking that the prince and the princess were destined to live in superficial bliss for all the days of their lives. Indeed, the tales of midlife invite us to develop ourselves by exploring those roles and opportunities that we denied ourselves in establishing our initial identities. And most often, to develop ourselves we must engage in deep soul work. On the other hand, when depression arises, we are encouraged to get over it, snap out of it, and be ourselves again.

Yet depression is one of the ways we go to the depths. When I was working with that group of bankers, near the end of our week-long workshop on career and life transitions, we were involved in creating a sociogram to see how the group was managing change. Each day, we had asked the same set of questions and invited people to place themselves on a scale of 1 to 10 (with 1 being danger and 10 being opportunity) in relation to each question. When that last question was asked, a voice responded from across the room. A teller who was being replaced by an ATM (automated teller machine) asked, "Where do you put sadness on that scale?" And someone else answered, "Sadness is what you ride to wisdom." What a wonderful truth. So often we chase sadness and depression away. Clinical depression deserves medical treatment—Prozac or Zoloft or lithium. But many times, these drugs are too hastily prescribed so that we can get over it rather than work through it.

In my own case, during the early days and nights of my mid-life passage, I was clearly depressed. I had several of the classic indicators, but the one I remember best was "loss of libido"—I had slipped into a flat, inert, lifeless state. Not only my sexual energy had dissipated but also my life force. The French use the phrase *elan vital*. The Welsh language, which is the language of my forebears, calls it *hywl*, which means "spirit," "vitality," "zest for life," "the spring in one's walk," "the vibrancy of voice," and even "the passion in one's loving." When I was in the midst of the forest of midlife, I had clearly lost my *hywl*.

My father died during my midlife passage. My brother and I were at his side for the last days, singing the great old Welsh hymns of pilgrimage and love—*Cwm Rhondda* ("Guide Me, O Thou Great Redeemer") and *Aberystwyth* ("Jesus, Lover of My Soul"). When Dad died, we arranged his funeral with much hymn singing and a special message, delivered in Welsh to my father, and interpreted in English for the rest of us. The messenger spoke of Dad's great *hywl*.

The day after the funeral I came back to my empty house and my empty life (I was separated from wife and family), but I put my suit on and headed off to work. When I was about a block away from my office, I turned and went back to the empty home, asked my associate to clear my schedule because I needed some solitude, and began three days of grieving. I created a scrapbook that traced my family and myself back for generations. I laughed some; cried a lot. And wrote words that helped me navigate myself through the despair of midlife. "The preacher used the Welsh word *hywl* to describe Dad. Exuberance or enthusiasm or zest. Well, Dad did have *hywl*, that's for sure. And I have had it too, but now in the midst of this separation and my painful wandering, I seem to have lost my *hywl*. I hope I can find that in myself again. I believe I can." When I lost my *hywl*, I sought some relief—even relief in the form of medication. But wise voices—including my therapist, several caring friends, and a voice from within—encouraged me to see this loss of *hywl* as a necessary stage in the process of deepening myself.

One day I was walking with a friend who was then a Roman Catholic missionary. We were walking by a stream—a pretty little babbling brook. Suddenly I noticed that the stream seemed to disappear. I commented on its absence. My friend said, "Don't worry, it's gone deeper. It'll come back, wait and see. And then it'll be even stronger." Sometimes in the early stages of this process, powerful and perplexing vacillations appear. Now one is sullen, one's spirit is subdued and *hywl* is absent. In the next moment, almost as if that *hywl* has suddenly hit a pool of energy, it bursts forth in a strangely agitated fashion. Whether on the surface or running underground, the soul's river is there.

Once I was leading a day-long workshop on career and life transitions for the local chamber of commerce. This brief workshop was not the environment for assisting persons in dealing with deep issues. Nevertheless, one man had obviously stepped into the soul's river, but was still at the earliest stages when agitation is typical. He sat silently for most of the morning, almost withdrawn from the group. Midway through the afternoon he began to break out of the back eddy where he had taken himself. He began muttering, "I must but I can't. I must but I can't." And then his voice began to rise and his spirit began to be agitated. "I must but I can't! *I must but I can't!*"

Finally, I asked him what was going on. "This is a career and life transition workshop, right?" he asked. "Well, let me tell you about my career and my life. I am an ophthalmologist. I built my practice from nothing. Now it is well established. I mean there are these big billboards with my picture on them. This is my life!" He paused. "And it's also my prison. I have twelve people who depend on my being dependable. My receptionist, my nurses, two of them, my bookkeeper, my office manager, my partners. I cannot leave them." Looking downward, he paused again. "And I have a family, a wonderful family. My wife has her own career, which is new and exciting, but does not bring in much money yet. And now the kids are in college. The first is in Dartmouth, the other three follow in the next few years. I cannot leave them."

I was confused about who he was thinking of leaving. So I asked, "Are you talking about leaving your family or your job?" He turned to me. "No, no, no. I'd never leave my family. Never. And I'd never leave my job. They're like family. In fact, in some ways they're more family than my family. I cannot leave them. Everyone is counting on me to be there. I cannot leave. But I cannot look another person in the eye."

This man said so much in those few words. On the one hand, he cannot leave his family, and he cannot leave his job because his staff are like family. But, on the other hand, he cannot look another person in the eye. He clearly had to make some major changes in his life if he was to have integrity—to look another person in the eye.

Another incident occurred as part of a real rite of passage ceremony, where men were able to be vulnerable with one another and able to struggle more fully with life's issues. A doctor in the group shared his struggles. "I've built this practice. I've built this reputation. I've built this image of myself as a fine doctor, a fine family man, a fine human being. But I'm sick at heart. I've got to change something, but I just can't." Almost the exact same phrase that we heard from the ophthalmologist, "I must but I can't."

Immediately I feared that this second man would break out of his impasse (I must but I can't) and get pushed in the wrong direction. If a doctor leaves his medical practice, the world will say, "What's wrong with Tom? Is he crazy?" But if a doctor leaves his wife and family, the world will say, "He probably outgrew her. There must have been some problems there we could not see. It takes two to tango." So the midlife passage gets played out once again. He has an affair. He divorces his wife and marries his new love. This is tragic. Unless this entire process is part of a more comprehensive growth pattern, he not only hurts himself and learns little, but he hurts his children, and he hurts his wife.

EMPTINESS OF SOUL AS OPPORTUNITY

Spouses get used and bruised during midlife. And men get vilified. We attack each other in the ongoing gender war. This is one of the places where partners need to help each other. And part of the way we can help each other is to see how we are different. A wise old woman, Bani Shorter, is a Jungian analyst. With a twinkle in her eye she speaks the great truth of the genders at midlife, indeed in so much of life: "We women embody life. You men act upon it."[9] Think about how that truth shapes our midlife experience. Women go through a change of life, called *menopause,* when their bodies actually change. This process stretches out, in most cases, for years. Although it has its individual variations, it is nevertheless an experience common to all women. The female midlife passage is *embodied.*

Men have no such thing. Men's bodies change, of course, but there is no male menopause, at least not in anything approaching the form that women experience. Furthermore, women's bodies have natural rhythms at work in them all the time. To create life, they embody that potential. And so they have cycles, periods. And with those periods come, for many, changes in moods. For all the disparaging comments men have made about "women on the rag," we should apologize and notice that women learn to live with changing moods, with the natural flow of life–giving blood, with the fluctuations of *hywl* or *elan vital* or libido, the life–giving spirit. Women learn, at least by adolescence, to recognize complex, vacillating feelings.

Robert Bly talks about this difference between women and men:

In high school a girl might ask, "Do you love me?" I couldn't answer. If I asked her the same question, she might reply, "Well, I respect you, I admire you, and I'm fond of you, and I'm even interested in you, but I don't love you." Apparently when she looked into her chest, she saw a spectrum of affections, a whole procession of feelings, and she could easily tell them all apart. If I looked down into my chest, I saw nothing at all. I had then either to remain silent or fake it.[10]

How terrifying to look into one's interior and find nothing there, or to go daily to a job that stopped yielding its satisfactions years ago, or to be in a marriage that has lost its excitement, or to feel as if everything is caught up in one vast system of indifference. William Blake, that genius of the soul, saw this same emptiness centuries ago. In those days corporations were called chartered companies. So pervasive was their influence, their enervating influence, that it was as if the whole world had become like a big chartered company.

When men feel this emptiness and experience this agitation of the soul, we often lack the patience to wait for our souls to be renewed and we often lack the ability "to ride sadness to wisdom." Instead, just as Bani Shorter suggests, we start *acting* upon life. We act as if we know our problem and we move aggressively to "solve" it without ever seeing the many opportunities for new life that lie hidden in our "problem."

Much better we follow Rainer Maria Rilke's wise advice to the young poet: "Be patient toward all that is unsolved . . . and try to love the *questions themselves*. . . . Do not now seek the answers, which cannot be given you because you would not be able to live them. . . . *Live* the questions now. Perhaps you will then gradually . . . live along some distant day into the answer."[11]

But to live the questions we need some help in knowing what the big questions really are. So often as the society trivializes the midlife transformation, and as men accept that diminished notion of the process, we end up anguishing over the standard questions, which are, in the final analysis, puny: Should I leave my job? Should I leave my spouse? Should I cash in my chips and start all over?

INSIGHTS FROM CARL JUNG AND ALBERT EINSTEIN

To answer any of those questions—without seeing them as part of a much more dramatic and demanding process—is to miss the point. Carl Gustav Jung and Albert Einstein can help us get at the big questions of midlife. Each had been the focus of study earlier in my life. While in midlife, I drew upon their wisdom. Without these thinkers, I might have capitulated to all the voices around me and within me demanding that I give up: "Just name something as the cause of your confusion and become the Bill we all know and love once again."

I was sorely tempted to buy into the understanding of life that blames others for making one a victim. But the concepts of Jungian psychology and quantum physics would come back to remind me that life is not as simple as causality. "On the contrary," the voice seemed to say, "maybe you are in this mess for good reason. If you can hold on to the tension, then you just may know more about your self."

Jung wrote a lot about midlife. One of his most important observations is this:

> The worst of it all is that intelligent and cultivated people live their lives without even knowing of the possibility of such transformations. Thoroughly unprepared we take the step into the afternoon of life; worse still, we take this step with the false assumption that our truths and ideals will serve us as hitherto. But we cannot live the afternoon of life according to the program of life's morning; for what was great in the morning will be little at evening, and what in the morning was true will at the evening have become a lie.[12]

Einstein said something similar: "No problem can be solved from the same consciousness that created it."[13] From both, the magnitude of the task becomes evident. Midlife is not about leaving one's job or marriage. It is about changing one's consciousness, one's program of life.

Because these two geniuses have much to tell us about our midlife task, let us briefly recount Jung's story and even more briefly look at Einstein's legacy as a way to take us a major step forward—a quantum leap, if you will—toward seeing the midlife journey as a noble and necessary time of transformation.

Almost everyone knows that Jung was a Swiss psychiatrist whose ways of thinking about the unconscious have greatly influenced Western thought in the last part of this century. But not everyone knows that Jung suffered a midlife crisis of the magnitude of the biblical character Job.[14] Jung's biographers generally date the onset of the crisis as 1912 and see it lasting for ten years. To understand what occurred, we need to go back to 1911, when Jung was thirty-six years old. At that time he is happily married to Emma, daughter of a wealthy industrialist, and they have one child. Jung is professionally established—he has a flourishing private practice; he is lecturer at the University of Zurich; he is the president of the International Psychoanalytic Association and the heir apparent to Sigmund Freud himself.

Within a few years, all those signs of success were gone. The stable life structure he had worked so hard and so effectively to create in the first half of his life was shattered. In particular:

~ In 1912 he wrote a paper that took issue with Freud, causing that central relationship to become strained and then broken.

~ He lost his capacity for professional work, cutting his private practice back to the bare minimum and resigning his position at the University of Zurich.

~ He fell in love with one of his patients, the then twenty-three-year-old Antonia Wolf. Needless to say, this put severe pressure on his previously stable marriage, especially when he insisted on bringing his lover to Sunday dinner. But even though incredibly pressured, the marriage did not break. Emma and Carl Jung remained married, and the relationship with Toni Wolf lasted for over fifty years.

These are some of the external signs that things were falling apart. Far more important to Jung were the internal dynamics. As the shell that had provided shape and meaning for his life cracked, the unconscious was loosed upon him with unbelievable fury:

~ Immense self doubt as he began to question the most fundamental values to which he had given his life.

~ A terrifying encounter with what he came to call the shadow—the despairing, hidden side of the psyche, which is filled with images of death and corpses and demons of all sorts. This encounter scared him to the core, made him become more private, fearing that if he shared any of his experiences, he would be viewed as insane.

~ An utterly confusing relationship with what he came to call the anima. This relationship was activated and shaped by his affair with Toni Wolf, whom he called his *soror mystica* ("soul sister"), but it was clear that his anima was more than and different from Toni Wolf, even though she was in some fashion a manifestation of it.

Through all this turmoil, Jung battled to hold on to a center. "My enduring these storms was a question of brute strength," he wrote. But he became persuaded that he was driven to survive "these assaults of the unconscious" because he was "obeying a higher will." He had a mission. "I was committing myself to a dangerous enterprise not for myself alone, but for the sake of my patients. . . . It was then that I ceased to belong to myself but to many others also. . . . I myself had to undergo the original experience, and then try to plant the results of my experience in the soil of reality."[15]

What did Jung's great midlife struggles yield for us? A greater knowledge of the persona, the shadow, and the anima, all of which we are likely to encounter in our own midlife passages. But far more important, Jung set out the task for the second half of life—to establish a dialogue between the ego and the self. (In chapter 6, we will look more fully at the task of initiating the dialogue with the self.) Suffice it to say, the dialogue with the self represents a change in consciousness, which echoes Einstein's advice, "No problem can be solved with the same consciousness that created it."

When Albert Einstein was a young man, the scientific world had a mind-set that was shaped to a great extent by the thinking of Sir Isaac Newton. Sir Isaac Newton, a deeply religious man who believed in causality (the law of cause and effect), had asserted that every event is caused by some preceding event, going all the way back to the primal mover (God). God, who was the creator, created a wonderfully intricate world, like a cosmic clock, and started things ticking. Once launched, God then stepped back into the heavens to let the world tick away to its end. Thus one could trace causality without worrying about an interfering deity.

Although not as celebrated or influential as Sir Isaac Newton, another Englishman, Thomas Young, also helped shape the scientific mind. In 1803, he performed the famous double-slit experiment, which proved without a doubt that light is a wave.

A full century later Albert Einstein, a brilliant young physicist, burst upon the scene with a force rarely experienced in any field. As a child he perplexed his teachers so much that one teacher wrote on a report card, "Possibly retarded." He had a particularly difficult time with mathematics. But by the time he was in the early stages of adulthood, it was clear that he was a genius.

In 1905 he was only twenty-six years old, but he published five major papers in that year alone. The first, for which he received the Nobel Prize in 1921, was on the *quantum* nature of light. He theorized that light is comprised of *quanta*, or particles, which he called *photons*. It's as if a beam of light is really a stream of little bullets (photons). To prove his theory he referred to the phenomenon called the *photoelectric effect*. When light hits a surface of metal, it jars loose the atoms from the metal and sends them flying off. We can count these electrons and measure how fast they go flying off, not unlike a billiard ball hitting other balls and sending them flying.

If light were a wave, it would take a moment before the waves could break loose those atoms, but the photoelectric effect demonstrates that the atoms are loosed instantaneously. Moreover, dimming the light does not change the velocity, only the number of photons. Changing the light's color is the only way to change velocity. High-energy color (violet) sends electrons flying off at a great speed, while low-energy color (red) sends electrons flying at a slow speed. The dimmer the light, the fewer the photons that send the electrons flying. All of this was ample proof of the quantum nature of light. Light is a quantum.

But none of this disproves that light is a wave. So a paradox is at hand. Thomas Young proved that light was a wave; Albert Einstein proved that light is a particle, a photon. But Einstein never proved that Young was wrong. Sometimes I think this is Einstein's greatest contribution. Two truths do not make a falsehood. Two rights do not make a wrong. Light is not either this or that. Light is both this *and* that, both a wave *and* a particle.

An old Sufi saying comes to mind: "You think because you understand *one* you must understand *two*, because one and one make two. But you must also understand *and*."[16] Einstein's mind did not require that he resolve this apparent conflict between light being wave *and* particle. He accepted the paradox as two truths. Therefore, he was able to direct his attention right between those two truths and focus on the *and*.

EARLY STEPS IN MY TRANSFORMATION

What this digression into the lives of Jung and Einstein has to do with men at midlife may seem a bit mysterious. In fact, it might make sense only if I share an experience I had long before I personally entered the confusing wilderness of midlife. A man in our congregation came to me with a dilemma. After years of marriage, a marriage that had all the external signs of happiness and success, he had stumbled into a complex relationship with a woman at work. It was not a simple affair; he maintained that it was not sexual but deeply satisfying, and in many ways this extramarital relationship filled needs that his marriage could not. He was, nevertheless, profoundly guilty, unable to sleep, barely able to function.

Finally, in an effort to do everything he could to make things right, he went with his wife to meet with her psychotherapist. No sooner had he taken his seat than the therapist confronted him with her question: "The issue here is very simple. Are you having an affair?" Caught by surprise, he refused to answer. And his refusal was immediately interpreted as proof of his guilt. He left that office in a rage and came directly to mine. "I couldn't answer her question," he complained. "Now you need to help me. Is what I am having an affair?" I couldn't answer either. It was and it wasn't.

Time out. I am sure I did not think of Albert Einstein on that day. I certainly was not feeling particularly ingenious at that moment. But in retrospect I believe Einstein might have been asked the same question about light. "The issue is very simple. Is light a particle or a wave? Make up your mind. It has to be one or the other. It can't be both." But Einstein refused to answer the question.

His mind did not require him to resolve the cognitive dissonance of light being *both* wave *and* particle.

Consequently, Einstein was able to turn his attention to the *and.* He performed the double-slit experiment using photons. With increasingly sophisticated instruments he was able to beam photons through various apertures—a wide opening, then a narrow opening (a slit), then two slits (a double slit). In every case, even though each photon was free to go where it might, all of the photons acting together functioned just like the waves of the original double-slit experiment and created the shadow patterns that Thomas Young had predicted a century earlier. Now the mystery of the *and* can begin to raise its questions. How does each photon know where to go?

Next, Einstein complicated the situation further. He designed a mechanism that would allow him to shoot two photons at once, and when they were first shot, it was not clear whether they were headed toward double slits, or whether one of the two slits would instantaneously close, meaning they were headed toward a single slit. Surprisingly, the photons always got the message, or so it seemed, and communicated with one another, or so it seemed, and came through the slit or slits and hit the wall on the other side exactly as they were supposed to.

Now the question of the *and* began to have even clearer shape. How does the photon know whether there are two slits or just one slit? How does information get around so quickly? How does information about what is happening elsewhere get collected to determine what is supposed to happen here? Could there be some type of consciousness connecting all reality at the subatomic level? Could it be that our universe is inhabited by a conscious force, the great *and*?

Time in. As I sat in my office with my perplexed friend begging for some clarity—Was he having an affair?—I soon came to realize that the question had two right answers, yes *and* no. The real issue, I believe, is neither the yes nor the no, but the *and*—the need to know how both right answers were connected to one another, how the unconscious notions of the feminine were being reshaped and consequently were causing his confusing behavior and immense guilt. As we continued to talk, this man learned to go right through the center of the paradox, the pair of truths, and deepen his questions. Our behaviors are not the result of simple causalities. They are rather the outcropping of forces that work both upon us and within us. And those forces are, to a great extent, hidden from us.

My own midlife journey began when those forces were pushing so hard that I was losing control of myself. Day after day I tried to stay attentive to my responsibilities. Night after night, I tossed in lonely torment. Finally, when the torment became so great that I could not stand to be alone any longer, I sought out some way to break the loneliness. Like so many others, I came to see psychotherapy as the only way to go.

THE FOUR TASKS OF MEN AT MIDLIFE

I knew I wanted to work with a Jungian therapist, so I made appointments with three and prepared for my first visit. To say it simply, that initial session was a disappointment; I knew immediately that this man and I would not address the issues I needed. But I also knew that the entire process of psychotherapy—literally "therapy for the soul" (from the Greek words *therapeutica,* "to attend to," and *psyche,* "soul")—was going to be exciting. I knew this because on the night before that first appointment, I had a dream, and, as far as I can remember, it is the only dream I've had in which no people are present. In the dream are four arrows, each one perfectly balanced off the others. For the longest time, no movement occurred at all; the system remained perfectly balanced.

Then one tiny arrow entered the picture. It gently approached one of the big arrows and nudged it, ever so slightly, off center. This then put pressure on the next arrow, which then exerted even greater pressure on the next, and so on. I woke up in a panic because by now the entire system was spinning out of control. All I could think of was a poem that I had memorized more than twenty years before when I was a sophomore in college—W. B. Yeats's "Second Coming":

> Turning and turning in the widening gyre
> The falcon cannot hear the falconer;
> Things fall apart; the centre cannot hold;
> Mere anarchy is loosed upon the world,

The blood–dimmed tide is loosed, and everywhere
The ceremony of innocence is drowned;
The best lack all conviction, while the worst
Are full of passionate intensity.

Surely some revelation is at hand;
Surely the Second Coming is at hand.
The Second Coming! Hardly are those words out
When a vast image out of *Spiritus Mundi*
Troubles my sight: somewhere in the sands of the desert
A shape with lion body and the head of a man,
A gaze blank and pitiless as the sun,
Is moving its slow thighs, while all about it
Reel shadows of the indignant desert birds.
The darkness drops again; but now I know
That twenty centuries of stony sleep
Were vexed to nightmare by a rocking cradle,
And what rough beast, its hour come round at last,
Slouches toward Bethlehem to be born? [17]

Several years later, when my life really had spun out of control, I had another dream that taught me more about the four arrows. In the dream I am a young boy walking with an older man to a square of some old Mexican Indian village. The old man says to me, "There is a great waterfall in the center of the square. It has all the energy in the world. It gives off a spray and a great deal of noise. We will be in a fog. There will be a terrible din. You will not be able to see me, except dimly through the fog, and you will not be able to hear me. For that matter you will not be able to hear yourself think. But if you can get all the way around the square and back to this road, all the energy of the waterfall will be yours." The old man continues: "There are four roads that enter the square, which you will soon see is really more of a circle. It would be best if you started out to your right. But you may find that you have to go against the traffic. No matter what, I will be with you, but you will not see me or hear me."

I have often recorded my dreams without having any idea what they meant. Now, years later, looking at life from a different perspective, I believe I can see their meaning more clearly. The ar-

rows are forces that have the capacity to pierce to the heart of the matter. They awaken eros, like Cupid's arrows. They hurt. They leave wounds. They point out the way for us. Four is the quaternity—north, south, east, and west—the number of wholeness. The square that is really a circle is a mandala, again, a symbol of wholeness.

The old man is the wise one. The boy is the innocent. The waterfall at the center is the great, dynamic energy system of all life. If we can get all the way around the circle, the energy of the waterfall will become ours. It *would* be best if we started out to our right, that is, if we addressed the issues of midlife in a certain sequence. Unfortunately, most of us take the issues in precisely the wrong order, going against the flow. Then we end up apologizing for everything. "*Lo siento,*" we say. "Please, pardon me." No matter what we say, we hear the scowling of the people complaining that we are messing up by going the wrong way.

Murray Stein's *In Midlife: A Jungian Perspective* taught me the identities of those four roads that radiate out from the center, and in identifying those roads, he introduced me to the four soul tasks of men at midlife. Stein speaks about those tasks this way:

> Jung describes the breakdown of the *persona,* a psychological structure that is the approximate equivalent of what Erikson calls psychosocial *identity,* accompanied by the release of two hitherto repressed and otherwise unconscious elements of the personality: the rejected and inferior person one has always fought becoming (the *shadow*), and behind that the contrasexual "other," whose power one has always, for good reason, denied and evaded (the *animus* for a woman, the *anima* for a man).[18]

Dealing with this breakdown and then the release of these powerful forces can be exceedingly threatening, and the threat can produce a protective reaction, what Jung calls "the reconstitution of the persona," the retreat back to the familiar patterns of identity.

Conversely, if we can find the courage to continue the journey through this terrifying psychological wilderness, we can arrive at the banks of the soul's river, which now we cross to engage the program of the second half of life, the discovery of the self. Murray Stein describes the goal of the journey in this way: "What one can gain from going all the way through the midlife transition, then, is a sense of an internal non-egoistic self and the feeling of integrity and wholeness that results from living in conscious contact with it. The midlife transition and crisis, then, involve making this crucial shift from a persona-orientation to a self-orientation."

Now we begin to see the terrifying terrain of midlife. There are four major soul tasks to be accomplished: (1) the breakdown of the persona; (2) the encounter with the shadow; (3) the encounter with the anima; and (4) the initiation of the dialogue with the self.

The old man in the dream was right when he said it would be best to deal with these four soul tasks "starting out to the right," that is, to deal with them in the order in which they have been listed. This order provides support so that men can address the sense of entrapment in their identities that so many men feel. But, unfortunately, men in midlife deny such feelings, even to themselves. So we will most likely be gripped by the shadow (those hidden and dismal parts of our soul) or the anima (those feminine erotic parts of our being). We shouldn't expect society's support. In fact, if we are going to be honest with ourselves, we should expect its wrath. We can excuse ourselves. But everyone will still be furious with us for going against the flow.

Perhaps this is the time to unfold my map of this territory, which is quite different from Daniel Levinson's. His shows us moving through several transitional stages as we progress from box to box to box. Every time I see his chart I feel a touch of despair. Who wants to risk the trials of midlife if you just end up in another box? Who wants to go through the whole of life jumping from one box to another?

My understanding of the midlife process is quite different because my own experience, as well as the experience of many men who have shared with me the stories of their journeys, is quite different. My map has one major transition—what I have called the grand mal of all life's transitions and what is often called the midlife crisis—which leads from the familiar box to a very different state of existence.

We know what the box is. It is the identity that each man has shaped and been shaped by. It is the program for the morning of our lives. Ask a question, get an answer. With every affirmative answer the identity becomes more secure. The box becomes more restrictive.

At some point the box breaks and we head out on an uncertain journey. We wander, seemingly aimless, seemingly out of control. There are times when it feels as if we are headed backward and other times when we feel utterly lost. This is the shadowland of midlife, the places of despair about which we would just as soon know nothing. At other times, we are drawn off course, as voyagers have been throughout time, by the seductive sounds of the feminine sirens (the anima).

But those who persevere emerge from the wilderness to a place with a new dynamic state, which I envision as a sphere or a wheel that is capable of rolling on and on as we "grow younger day by day to our death." Unlike the box, in which we derive our identity by focusing on the periphery, the cutting edge between the I and the Not-I, in the dynamic state which we discover when we accomplish the midlife transition, our focus is on the center of the wheel. We derive our sense of self from the core values of our being.

The midlife passage is not just an intimacy or vocational crisis. It is not just a matter of breaking out of one box and rushing into another. The real midlife passage beckons us to wander through the wilderness until we arrive at and begin crossing the soul's river, willing to open ourselves to utterly new truths about ourselves, our relationships, our faith. It asks us to live with uncertainty. It begs us not to try to solve every problem the moment it is presented. It pleads with us not to run from the dangers hidden beneath the surface of the river but to follow the currents of the river, the inner logic of this period in our life, until we are allowed to uncover the hidden opportunities that await us at the end of the journey.

2

FORGING THE RITE OF PASSAGE FOR MEN

Men need a rite of passage to guide them on their midlife journey. I came to this conclusion over a number of years. Long before I was old enough to enter the wilderness of midlife, I led men's groups. Furthermore, I counseled with men who were stumbling through midlife. Not infrequently those men were fathers of adolescents who were in the initiation group—our congregation's rite-of-passage-to-adulthood group. These fathers would tell me it would have been helpful if they had a structured experience like their children's.

While sitting in a darkened Broadway theater watching Peter Shaffer's prize-winning play *Equus*, I came to the conclusion that someone needed to create this rite. The play has three main characters. Martin Dysert is a middle-aged doctor in a psychiatric hospital in southern England who, like so many of his professional colleagues, is intrigued with things primitive. Alan Strang is a patient in the hospital because he blinded six horses with a steel spike and because he claimed to be worshiping them. Hester Salomon is a magistrate who is also Martin's confidante and companion; she listens to him as he searches for his self. Two other personalities are important to this play. One is a horse named Nugget, onto whom Alan Strang projects his overwhelming need to worship. The other is Margaret Dysert, a dentist who is also Martin's wife, on whom he projects the remainder of his unconscious material.

At one point in the drama the interplay between doctor and patient is such that Martin begins to see the emptiness of his own life. He tries, as so many men do, to blame that emptiness on his wife, but the unblinking look of his patient forces him to look more deeply into himself. Slowly Martin begins to realize what he has done to himself. In order to become successful he has given up his capacity to feel his own pain. "Look . . . to go though life and call it yours—your life—you first have to get your own pain. Pain that's uniquely yours. You can't just dip into a common bin and say, 'That's enough!'" he says to himself in Hester's presence.

In order to be accepted as the professional he purports to be, he has given up his own passion. "That boy has known a passion more ferocious than I have felt in any second of my life. And let me tell you something. I envy him."[1] In order to be everything a thoughtful and objective psychiatrist is expected to be, Martin has given up his worship. At first he blames even this on his wife:

> Mentally, she's always in some drizzly kirk of her own inheriting; and I'm in some Doric temple—clouds tearing through pillars—eagles bearing prophecies out of the sky. She finds all that repulsive. All my wife has ever taken from the Mediterranean—from that whole vast intuitive culture—are four bottles of Chianti to make into lamps, and two china condiment donkeys labeled Sally and Peppy.
>
> I wish there was one person in my life I could show. One instinctive, absolutely unbrisk person I could take to Greece, and stand in front of certain shrines and sacred streams and say, "Look. Life is only comprehensible through a thousand local Gods. And not just the old dead ones with names like Zeus—no, but living Geniuses of Place and Person. And not just Greece but modern England! Spirits of certain trees, certain curves of brick wall, certain chip shops, if you like, and slate roofs. I'd say to them, 'Worship as many as you can see—and more will appear!'" . . .
>
> If I had a son, I bet you he'd come out exactly like his mother. Utterly worshipless.[2]

But the relentless stare of his pained, passionate, worshipful patient demands that Martin look at himself. And this is what he sees:

I go on about my wife. That smug woman by the fire. Have you thought of the fellow on the other side of it? The finicky, critical husband looking through his art books on mythical Greece. What worship has *he* ever known? Real worship. Without worship you shrink, it's as brutal as that. . . . I shrank my *own* life. No one can do it for you. I settled for being pallid and provincial, out of my own eternal timidity.[3]

And finally, he is able to look at his own calling, psychiatry, and see the mistake so many of us make. In the name of respectability, he has lost his life. Hester, his companion, tries to comfort him by arguing that the boy's stare is not an accusation, but something quite different. "He's not accusing you. He's claiming you." "For what?" Martin asks. And she answers mischievously, "For a new God." Martin responds with a great insight. "Too conventional, for him. Finding a religion in psychiatry is really for ordinary patients."[4]

MEN NEED WORTHY RITUALS

This insight points to one of the great dilemmas for modern men at midlife. We need rites of passage to help us traverse the soul's river, and when we cannot find them, we turn to psychotherapy. But psychiatry offers too weak a soup. Norman O. Brown and Joseph Campbell see our problem very clearly. Brown says, "Religious remnants of such practices still exist; but they have now shrunk to historical, isolated relics out of step with the schedules of status change in all other areas of modern life."[5]

Campbell sees the same thing:

There can be no question, the psychological dangers through which earlier generations were guided by the symbols and spiritual exercises of the mythological and religious inheritance, we must face alone, or at best, with only tentative, impromptu, and not too often very effective guidance. . . . [This is our problem as modern] enlightened individuals, for whom all the gods and devils have been rationalized out of existence.[6]

Two other writers—James Hollis and Murray Stein—decry this loss in our life and focus their attention specifically on the midlife transition:

> The popularity of Gail Sheehy's *Passages* a few years ago testifies to the importance of the theme of periodic change. Yet, our culture has lost the mythic road map that helps locate a person in a larger context. Without a tribal vision of the gods, and their spiritual network, modern individuals are cut adrift to wander without guidance, without models, and without assistance through the various life stages. Thus, the Middle Passage, which calls for the death before rebirth, is often experienced in frightening and isolating ways, for there are no rites of passage and little help from one's peers, who are equally adrift.[7]

Murray Stein notes the rise of psychotherapy to take the place of religion in this transition process:

> Midlife is a transitional period within the life span as a whole. This transition can be regarded as homologous to transitions that the initiation rituals of so-called primitive peoples are designed to facilitate. The psychological purpose of this transition seems to be the transformation of consciousness, and while modern society seems to lack a suitable ritual process for going through this transition period, psychotherapy is increasingly performing this function.[8]

I argue that therapy cannot fill the vacuum left by the loss of rites of passage. I see therapists trying their best. Conferences purport to train therapists for this role. Journal articles discuss the task at length. Well-meaning practitioners describe their work in terms of a rite of passage. Although it may be easy to view the therapeutic process as something *like* a rite of passage, it is not an actual rite of passage.

In contrast, I have witnessed the effectiveness of worship as a rite of passage. During seminary I served as a chaplain at Wiltwick School for Boys. Every weekend I led worship for 150 so-called juvenile delinquents, who entered into that experience of worship so completely that all through Advent they *became* shepherds wandering around in the dark trying to find a baby who might be the Christchild. By Easter they had become Roman guards, confused and angry that some SOB had rolled the stone away from the tomb. As weeks shaped themselves into seasons, and seasons shaped themselves into years, and those great legendary figures from the past came alive in adolescents of the present, I could see transformation.

Robert Bly speaks of this process of transformation:

> Every man and woman on this planet is on the road from the Law to the Legends. . . . We are each on the way from dogma to Midrash, from the overly obedient men to wildness. . . . The Law stands for the commandments we need in order to stay alive, the rules that say which side of the road to drive on, the law of gravity. The Legends stand for the moist, the swampish, the wild, the untamed. The Legends are watery when compared with the dryness of the Law. It takes twenty years to understand the Laws, and then a whole lifetime to get from there to the Legends.[9]

Part of the reason I once delighted in leading worship for so-called juvenile delinquents, I am sure, is that they did not have a lot of respect for the law. But they were really open to the legends. And part of the reason I now delight in creating rituals for men at midlife is that the men ripest for transformation are a lot like those adolescents. In most cases, we did not rebel when we were adolescents. Now in midlife the anima beckons, and we find ourselves walking in the shadowland. We do not need laws to tell us where we went wrong. We need legends and legendary figures to be our guides so that we find our own way.

We also need a community of men. The ancient Chinese knew this well. The *I Ching* speaks about the growth process:

> Times of growth are beset with difficulties. They resemble a first birth. But these difficulties arise from the very profusion of all that is struggling to attain form. Everything is in motion: therefore if one perseveres there is a prospect of great success. . . . Likewise, it is very

important not to remain alone: in order to overcome the chaos he needs helpers.[10]

MEN NEED ONE ANOTHER TO MAKE THE CROSSING

Two of my friends entered the wilderness of midlife and, before they could complete their journeys, were tragically killed in separate accidents. One was named Jon. We went to college together and twice traveled through Mexico with our college choir. After graduation Jon went off to India, where he made a name for himself as a performer of the intricate and mysterious music of South India. One of his albums describes him as "the Pavarotti of Indian music."

We were reunited as adults and became squash partners and close companions. One year he took a sabbatical leave and traveled to India for a concert tour. Afterward he came for a visit. At breakfast the first day, he reported that he did not sleep well. Indeed, it was the first of many nights when he did not sleep well. Jon had begun the journey of midlife. And for him it would be a demanding journey. He had the best of psychiatric care. He had the latest in psychotherapeutic drugs. But Jon needed still more; he needed helpers, friends, companions; he needed a community.

As his insomnia continued, he used to call me, sometimes very late at night, to ask if he could come over to talk. And we would talk, but he also yelled and screamed, ranted and raved. I would do my best to calm him. When he settled down, he would thank me for being with him. I would say, "Don't thank me, Jon. My turn's coming. And when it comes, promise me that you'll be there for me, because you're simply going down this road before me."

Jon would promise. And I know he would have been there. But even though he had pretty much made it through his midlife passage, late one Friday night, when he was walking his dog, he didn't make it home. He was hit by a drunk driver and killed.

I'm certain that his death contributed to the onset of my midlife crisis. But even more, I'm sure that the loss of this friend who had already made the journey made my passage much more perilous. When the nights came, no men were there with whom to talk. Married men would meet with me over lunch. But by evening those men were home with their wives and children. And I was alone.

Part of the reason many men do not have supportive friends is that we are frightened by male friendship gatherings. We are afraid we might be considered either gay or overly macho types. Thus men in midlife are alone—at the very time we need community.

We also need action. The famous Toni Wolf, Jung's paramour when she was in her twenties, remained close to him until his death. She was a greatly valued analyst at the Jung Institute in Zurich. She apparently had little patience for people who just wanted to think and talk about stuff that presented itself from the unconscious. She demanded action. "What did you *do* about that dream from last week?" she would ask. If they had not acted, then she would send them back out the door and explode, "Come back when you mean business." She explained, "People can analyze for twenty years and nothing below the neck is aware that anything is going on! You have to do something about it! Do something with your muscles!"[11]

Whenever I think about that call to action, my friend Stu comes to mind. For years he was my tennis partner, but before that he was a class athlete, captain of his football team at Williams College and All New England. He explained to me that he was a pulling guard—generally someone who is big, strong, and fast who, when the ball is snapped, can plow ahead of the ball carrier, leading the action, blocking any would-be tacklers out of the way. Stu was just such an athlete.

After college, Stu saw some gruesome action in Vietnam as an intelligence officer with the Montagnards. Upon his return, Stu became an educator, first as a counselor at a home for delinquent adolescents and eventually as a high school principal. Principals have a lot of laws to follow and enforce. I'm sure Stu did all of that, but he also managed to become a legend in that high school. Each February he would dress up to become George Washington and read the Declaration of Independence. Once, to raise money for the parent-teacher organization, he volunteered for mud wrestling. Stu was a man of action.

Stu was active in our church. He volunteered for all types of projects—the greater the challenge, the greater his eagerness to get involved. Whenever things slowed down, Stu had ingenious ways of letting us know. When a fellowship supper dragged on too long, Stu might pull the vacuum out from the storage closet and start cleaning up. Or, should a sermon become tedious, Stu might loosen his tie, then pull it off, and—if the sermon were not rushing to a finish, he would start unbuttoning his shirt, button by button, until the preacher got the message.

In the midst of this active life, Stu went through a sudden and terrible change. While he was visiting colleges with his teenage daughter, which was surely a time for reflecting on the passing of life, he had an attack of diverticulitis that nearly killed him. He was given a temporary colostomy and confined to bed, first in the hospital and then at home, for a long time. Day after day, night after night, as he handled the shit of his life, both literally and figuratively, he began to go through the early stages of the midlife passage. He initiated counseling with a skillful psychotherapist, and I have no doubt that it was good. He was administered the latest drugs, and I have no doubt that these were helpful. But Stu needed more. He was not an ordinary patient; he was a man of action. He needed more than talk therapy or pharmacological solutions. He needed to *do* something.

Tragically, one Saturday morning, as he walked alone with his thoughts, he was hit by a speeding car and killed. With the shocking news of Stu's death, I saw many of our mutual friends and listened to their experience of his illness and death. Time and again I heard, "When Stu got so bad, I got scared. Frankly, when he got bad, I shied away." When he needed them the most, his friends backed away because they did not know what to say or do.

Stu was a man who needed action. Jon was a man who needed community. The rest of us are just like them.

BUILDING A RITE OF PASSAGE

I firmly believe that Jon and Stu would have benefited from a rite of passage appropriate for men at midlife. It would have given them a community of men. It would have given them action. It would have given them a relatively safe and structured way to connect with the great issues of their lives, which were rising up from the depths and demanding attention. It would have given them a way to worship.

Worship—the word comes from two Anglo–Saxon root words: *woerth*, which means "worth," and *scipe*, which generally means "the state of being or doing" and is used in such words as statesmanship or craftsmanship. So *worship* is the state of being or doing something that is ultimately worth it.

Primitive cultures placed worship at the center of their life. Primitive peoples probably did not spend a lot of time analyzing their worldviews. Modern scholars suggest that primitive peoples had two worlds of time: *primordial time*, original time, like a great circle going round and round since the beginning, when the gods were active on earth and when the order of all things was established; and *actual time*, like a vicious circle going round and round right now, a time when the holy is more distant because separation or the fall occurred and the primordial time receded.[12]

Actual time in this worldview is basically worthless. The gods are not here. The important truths are not here; they are already established as laws. The holy or other forces that give meaning are not here. The profane is here. Despair and death are here. And insignificant humans doing insignificant things are here.

Primordial time has receded, but it still exists—hidden, enfolded, masked by the shadows of actual time. Humans are prevented from seeing it, but the shadows cannot quite extinguish it. The light shines in the shadows, and the shadows cannot overcome it.

This wisdom of primitive peoples finds a certain resonance with a fascinating concept from contemporary physics—implicate, or enfolded, order—developed by David Bohm, one of the world's most influential quantum mechanical physicists and philosophers. I introduce this intriguing concept in presentations on men at midlife with a show-and-tell demonstration using a bubble of ink in a cylinder of glycerin.

The demonstration begins when we drop the ink bubble into the glycerin. At first the glycerin holds the ink in its bubble shape, but when the cylinder is rotated, faster and faster, the ink drop begins to draw out longer and longer until it's a very thin thread. Then it disappears completely; nobody can see it; it's gone.

But when the cylinder is spun in the opposite direction, the thread of ink reappears and gradually grows back into the shape of the original drop. When the ink is invisible to us, it is enfolded in the glycerin, implicit in the broader order. When it becomes visible again, it is unfolded, explicit.

The concept of implicate order implies that all reality functions as a constant interplay between the *visible* (the explicate, the unfolded) and the *invisible* (the implicate, the enfolded). The visible is evident; the invisible is not. But the visible is actually shaped by the invisible. The ancient definition of a sacrament fits this interplay: the outward and visible sign of an inward and invisible grace.

Primitive peoples knew how the invisible, implicate, enfolded order related to the visible, explicate, unfolded order. They knew that the light was in the shadows. They knew this meaningless actual time could have meaningful primordial time represented. They knew all of this because they did it. They did it by using myth and ritual.

Plato had a similar understanding of the nature of reality. He maintained that our current knowledge springs from a treasury of memory, which we constantly draw upon but which we cannot in a single stroke bring to the fore. He was so convinced of this that he postulated a former life where we would have had an immediate vision of truth. Thus, according to him, all our apparent discoveries are nothing but recollections stirred up in us by the images of eternal ideas that we encounter in the visible world.

Plato used the word *recollection;* the primitives, and for that matter the ancient Hebrews and the early Christians, used the word *re-member.* The Passover Seder is a meal of remembrance. The Eucharist is a time when Christians eat and drink, and this they do in remembrance of their Christ. A member is something that has an intimate, even organic union with a larger entity. My hand is a member of my body. I am a member of a family or a congregation or a corporation. I am one of it. I am one with it. And to re-member means to be one with it again.

The way primitive people re-membered themselves was through worship. They gathered in community. They retold the stories of the primordial times, the myths that shape all life. As they told the stories they brought them to life through their rituals. They used their muscles, their actions, to re-member themselves with the community that stretched from the time before time all the way to the end, from alpha to omega.

The ancient Hebrews were so skilled at entering this time that their language has an unusual verb tense, *vev,* the worship (or historical) present. When we enter into the full experience of worship, we know *ecstasy,* literally "standing outside of time." The past, the future, and the present all merge into one state of being that might be called the *eternal now.* When we experience the eternal now, the hidden truths reveal themselves, the implicate order of things unfolds itself, the light shines through the gloom.

Rites of passage were designed by primitive peoples as guides from one state of existence to another. That time between the times, when we are betwixt and between, is *liminal* time. Because we are disconnected from our usual anchors, we become receptive in liminal time to eternal truths that otherwise would elude us. Rites of passage turn the cylinder of time in the other direction so that the implicit becomes explicit.

Modern rites of passage can only benefit from what we learn about the rites of primitive peoples. The three basic lessons are these: First, all rites of passage—whether they mark the passage from nonlife to life (birth), from childhood to adulthood (initiation), from living life as individuals to living as the two–becoming–one (marriage), or from life to afterlife (death)—have a classic structure of three parts, namely, separation, transition, reincorporation. Second, each part of the total rite can also echo these three parts. Third, each of life's rites of passage has its own purpose and content.

The rite of passage for men at midlife addresses four soul tasks:

~ Breakdown of the persona
~ Encounter with the shadow
~ Encounter with the soul mate
~ Initiation of the dialogue with the self

In addressing these four soul tasks, we are not just going to talk about them. We are not primarily concerned about making prudent decisions. We certainly will not be satisfied by simply knowing what others think about these issues. In our rite of passage we will try to *worship* our way to a deeper level. We will risk letting go of the present, enter the eternal now, and know ourselves in radically new ways.

Each soul task has a legendary figure, a soul brother, who will walk with us for part of our journey. We will ask questions of these brothers, question after question until our questions have a life of their own and we discover that we truly can live the questions . . . until they give us back their wisdom.

For each soul task a mystery rite will help us get beyond our tendency to focus on life as a set of problems to be solved, so that we can experience life as a mystery to be lived. The first of these mystery rites (the breakdown of the persona) will be explained in considerable detail. The second two (the encounter with the shadow and the soul mate, or anima) will be offered with less detail. The final mystery rite (initiating dialogue with the self) will be briefly sketched. By this time, the community of men should be sufficiently formed so that a natural liturgy can emerge from the group. The word *liturgy* is constructed from two Greek words: *leit*, which means "the people," and *ergon*, which means "work" or "energy." So true liturgy always draws upon the natural energies of the group and shapes those energies into worship forms. Now, before I go any further, I need to alert you to some problems.

TYPICAL OBJECTIONS

When this rite of passage for men at midlife is presented to groups, one of the first objections always is, "But isn't every man's midlife passage different?" This challenge usually masks a more pressing issue: "Is this a good thing to be doing? Should we be dignifying what men do at midlife by actually calling these things soul tasks?" The short answer to each question is yes. Yet taking each question seriously is important in order to foster a dialogue and the basis for a community.

Every man's midlife life passage is different. Some are short; some are seemingly endless. Some begin at thirty; some start after fifty. Some are little wrinkles in the fabric of life; some tear that fabric to pieces. So, how can we have a single rite of passage that will fit them all?

This same question is asked of all rites of passage. I often heard it asked of our adolescent rite of passage to adulthood. It is important to remember that *the rite* of passage is not the same thing as *the passage* itself. The initiation rite does not make an adolescent into an adult. At best, it helps someone become an adult and allows society to acknowledge the change. Change is a process, not an event. The changes characterized by adolescence go on for years. The initiation rite is a series of events that empower that process of change, making it safer, steadier, and deeper and allowing both the initiates and their world—family, friends, church, and community—to say, "Something is happening here," and eventually, "Something has happened here. One who was once a child is now an adult."

The process called adolescence is always longer than the rite of passage. Adolescence begins earlier and ends later. And furthermore, many of the most important transformative moments often occur far away from the supportive initiation group. I guess one could start an initiation rite of passage when the kids are about twelve and end it as late as the mid–twenties. But the fact is that the years in the middle—about age fourteen, fifteen, sixteen—seem best for a two–year initiation to adulthood.

The same issue applies to the midlife rite of passage. As long as the rite of passage is not mistaken for the passage itself, then the rite could be offered to men who are thirty or older. No upper limit can be set; I have had men in their sixties in groups. Each man can choose for himself when he is ready for his rite.

How long should the rite last? It could be a three–day retreat; it is powerful as an executive retreat for men who work together but rarely share deeply with one another. It could be a series of retreats. My favorite model stretches out over approximately seven weeks, beginning with a retreat that includes the rite of separation, followed by several weekly meetings to enter into great old stories that allow us to encounter the anima and the shadow, and concluding with a second retreat and a rite of reincorporation.

Finally, we turn to the more pressing objection. How appropriate is it to dignify what happens to men at midlife with something that actually looks like worship—implying that it is ultimately worthwhile? Men (especially group leaders) who are uneasy about this will need to examine their own attitude and whatever is prompting it. The most straightforward option is to pose this question to individuals or the group whenever considerable resistance is expressed.

Once at a conference, Rabbi Harold Kushner, author of *When Bad Things Happen to Good People*, talked about the challenge of being a therapist to people who offend one's sensibilities in some way.

His example was a counselor assigned to work with an obese woman. The therapy did not go very well, and when it was terminated the woman turned to the therapist and said, "I could tell all along that you never really liked me, that in fact you couldn't stand me."

Our attitudes, consciously or otherwise, always show through. The craziness of men in midlife is often far more offensive than obesity. One cannot create or lead this rite unless one can say, "For all the confusion and pain, this should be a time of growth and transformation, indeed, a *noble* and *necessary* time of growth and transformation."

PART TWO

THE FOUR SOUL TASKS FOR CROSSING

3

THE BREAKDOWN OF THE PERSONA

What is the persona of the men who face midlife? The generation from 1946 until 1960 was a tumultuous one. With World War II ended, military personnel and factory workers returned to their homes and families. It should not have come as any surprise that, beginning in 1946, the maternity wards were busy. A few years later the elementary schools were overcrowded, then the high schools, and eventually the colleges. When this generation, labeled the baby boomers, entered the workforce in the mid-1960s, the economy was strong. By the 1980s, when these postwar children were hitting their prime, the economy was also booming and could accommodate them, indeed, could celebrate their arrival and create a name for them—yuppie.

WHAT IS THE PERSONA?

The term *yuppie* is based on an acronym for three common attributes: (1) young, (2) urban, and (3) professional. In the early 1980s, when the term was coined, the baby boomers *were* young—from 20 to 35 years old. They were also urban, and even as they moved out of the cities and into the suburbs, they kept their urban attitudes—free from tradition, flexible, responsive, ready to take advantage of any opportunity for advancement. They were particularly drawn to large corporations, where they saw opportunities for promotions, a stable career path, and the promise of large rewards. The exchange, of course, was their readiness to relocate at the request of their employers, moving from one corporate subdivision to another.

Many observers have focused on the urban, cosmopolitan nature of this generation. Yet the most interesting aspect of the yuppie appellation is its third characteristic. A yuppie is *professional*. Originally the term *professional* was reserved for someone who had trained for one of the three classic professions, namely, law, medicine, or the church. Because each required application of a large body of knowledge to particular needs and circumstances, these professions required a lengthy training period. But over time, this definition was diluted. By the 1980s *professional* did not imply that a person had a certain educational degree; rather, it meant how persons looked and presented themselves, and it denoted a certain status.

How does one signal such status? One needs status symbols—tangible status symbols, such as luxury cars, big houses with impressive facades, even particular watches and ink pens. To get all these you need money—handsome compensation with generous perks. Then add intangible symbols, such as job titles, career opportunities, and recognition. Consequently, many yuppies were naturally drawn to the biggest corporations, with their promises of titles, career growth, and endless opportunities.

The classic American corporation has a well-defined structure. Usually it is shaped like a pyramid, with a big base of workers on the bottom and fewer managers or executives on each successive rung, until at the top is one person, generally the chief executive officer (CEO).

These men (and most are still male) live in boxes, much like the glass boxes that politicians are required to construct and inhabit. Although few would use this language system, the CEO is the spiritual head of the organization, the icon. Day after day, he puts on his suit, which like an actor's costume helps him play his role in a theatrical production of focus, direction, and control. These CEOs develop identities, or, rather, identities were developed for them. The system carves a mask for them and tells them to live out their lives within the confines of that mask.

In my work consulting with corporations, I frequently hear CEOs talk about the limitations imposed on them by their roles. In the privacy of our relationship they wonder what life would be like if they could take off their masks and be released from their roles. Sometimes they dare to step out of character, perhaps allowing the comforting images of masculine strength to show some cracks. When they do, the entire corporate system beams powerful forces to seal up the crack. This, of course, is a dramatic example of the persona.

JOB LOSS, OUTPLACEMENT, AND THE PERSONA'S BOX

Just as the preeminent organization man can illustrate persona, so the meteoric rise of a new industry called outplacement can illustrate corporate mask maintenance. The early 1980s, when the economy was booming and corporations were growing, saw little need for outplacement, not so much because few people were losing their jobs, but because outplacement was not needed to protect corporate images. But by the early 1990s, when the economy moved into its recession, the realities of corporate life began to change.

A new language system was created to mask this reality. The corporations—which formerly had laid off, cut back, or fired people they could no longer afford—began to "downsize" (later revised to "rightsize") and uncover "redundancies" that required "career adjustments" and the "outplacement" of those employees. And to further mark the reality of what was happening, the "severance packages" included "outplacement services."

When I joined the Big Eight accounting firm, my first assignment was to develop their "career transition consulting" practice. To seek out benchmarks and best practices, I visited our primary competitors, which had already established the cultural norms for this emerging industry. What I saw deeply distressed me. I had perhaps naively assumed that the goal was to help these newly unemployed persons take a fresh look at their lives, honestly assess how they had boxed themselves into their careers, and begin to envision new opportunities for themselves. The outplacement firms, in contrast, seemed to do everything they could to keep the lid on things, to keep the box sealed and on the conveyor belt. Typical bits of advice to newly terminated persons included the following:

~ "Make sure you look good. Dress up the same way you did every other working day and come *here* to work."

~ "You'll have an office here. You'll have access to phones and fax and a copying machine. You'll have a secretary. We'll do all we can to make this feel just like the office you went to before."

~ "You'll never get another job if you bad-mouth your former employer. We'll train you how not to express those negative feelings."

~ "We can teach you how to smile on the phone when you talk. That smile comes right through the phone lines."

~ "Try not to upset your spouse."

~ "Here, create a network of contacts and see if you can get a job just like the one you lost."

No doubt boiling down the weeks or months of assistance to these bits of advice oversimplifies the services provided. I also know that some helpful work gets done in outplacement offices. But when one follows the money, a fundamental truth emerges. Outplacement services are usually paid for by the corporations. And the abiding concern of every corporation is its image, its mask. Angry former employees tarnish that image. So it is best to keep the lid on things.

The loss of a job is not the same as the breakdown of the persona. Such a loss is just a crack in the shell. But to seal up the crack so quickly is a disservice to the humanity of that employee because it blocks the first soul task. This may seem like an extreme claim until one examines the first soul task more systematically.

The persona is described in various ways. Murray Stein says it is a psychological structure that is the approximate equivalent of Erikson's concept of identity. Daniel Levinson calls it the individual life structure. I have already referred to it simply as the box. The persona is the box. This box is not a bad thing but a necessary thing. Each of us needs a persona, a self-definition, an identity that we have negotiated with the world. This negotiation process begins soon after birth and intensifies during our adolescence and early adulthood.

A MASKING RITUAL FOR ADOLESCENTS

The rite of passage to adulthood helps the adolescent initiates at our church become intentional about forming an identity. Adolescents are encouraged to see their lives as a totality, from birth to death, apart from the fads of the moment. Each group talks with expectant parents. It witnesses a birth (using professional films and having parents explain the wonder of it all). We look at infancy and childhood, consider adolescence as a transitional time, ponder marriage, divorce, working for a living, retirement. And then we visit wise old people and conclude this overview of a whole life by attending a funeral.

During this introduction to the life cycle, several exercises help the initiates compose a life that fits best with their personality. By far the most powerful event is the masking rite, one of seven mystery rites that punctuate the entire initiation. This masking rite is adapted from cultures all over the world and from a classic pattern for making major decisions—opening one's self up to new possibilities and then choosing the possibility that seems consonant with one's present level of self-awareness.

Emerging adults in primitive societies are exposed, either actually or ritualistically, to a wide variety of experiences. They are encouraged to entertain as many possibilities for themselves as they can. The goal is to expand their self-concept. Then, at a critical point, they choose the one possibility that seems most compatible with themselves. Sometimes this is done by the initiates, sometimes by the initiators. Always it is done after the gods have been invoked and with the confidence that divine forces are participating in the decision, which is seen as a vocation, a calling, a destiny.

This process of arriving at an acceptable self-definition in primitive cultures is often accomplished with the aid of masks. The mask is the persona, the public representation of a personality. The heroic lives of the ancestors in the beginning offer a finite number of personalities. (The number is determined by the number of lives lived heroically and by the number of roles needed to keep society functioning.) The roles of the heroes can never be abandoned. They must be passed from one generation to another, as the life force of the older manifestation moves to the point of ineffectiveness.

At the time of decision, initiates are allowed to see the several masks presently available. They try them on to experience how they feel. Then they select or have selected for them the mask that best fits their personality. Once the mask has been assigned, the wearer of the mask experiences both grief and exhilaration—grief in knowing about the many options not chosen and exhilaration in exploring the implications of the selected persona.

In Africa, both the making and the wearing of the mask are activities partaking of the holy. Consequently, masks are protected with rites and taboos. Carving a mask requires fasting, sexual abstinence, and a sacrifice to prevent the carver from becoming a victim of the power that his creation draws to itself. This is especially true with death masks, used throughout the world in a final attempt to unmask the essence of a person.[1]

The power of the mask can also be seen through its use in Greco–Roman culture. The ancient Greeks used the mask to portray different *personae* ("characters") in their *theater* ("act of seeing, viewing"). An actor entered a mask and thereby became a person in the drama. The Romans adopted and developed this custom. The Latin word for mask is *larva*, a "ghost" or "apparition." (*Larva* also means "the immature form of animals that undergo metamorphosis"—their grub state before their transformation into a pupa, or pupil.) Young Roman men were told to "carve your mask," which meant that they were to develop their character, become their distinctive self.[2]

In our church's initiation program, the traditional use of masks, in both primitive cultures and Greco–Roman times, is described to the adolescents and enables them to use the masking ritual to assist them in the crucial task of forming an identity. They cannot do that in isolation. They need to negotiate the great questions of identity formation, such as, Who am I? Who will I be within this society? What has God intended me to do?

Our masking ritual for adolescents follows the tripartite pattern of all rituals—separation, transition, reincorporation. The initiates fast and then gather together for a final period of preparation by talking about character formation. I remember one occasion well. We were in a darkened room, keeping silence until a big question was asked, When does your identity get established? After a period of silence, several persons spoke:

> For me it was last year. Up until that time I was sort of a
> wise guy. Never did my work. Parents always on my case.
> You know what I mean. But last year I joined the swim

team, and I was good, to everyone's surprise. So now that I'm a success, I don't have to be a wise guy anymore.

It was much earlier for me. By the time I was in second grade, I was just like I am now.

My mother talks about my first day at school. She said I was the "kindergarten parent" within hours. I'm always taking care of people. That's just the way I am.

Funny you say that. My mother claims that when I was in the hospital after I was born, I was already doing what I still do—just lying there, smiling at the world, trying to get everyone's attention.

(A female co-leader then spoke up.) The character may be formed even earlier than that. I have two children. While they were still in the womb they had their personalities. She was active, kicking, full of life, ready to get on with it. He was peaceful, quiet, content to be where he was. They are both the same today.

Then words of Psalm 139 were read. The wisdom of the ages suggests that our identities may get formed still earlier yet:

O God, you have searched me and known me.
You know when I sit down and when I rise up;
 you discern my thoughts from far away. . . .
Even before a word is on my tongue,
 O God, you know it completely.
You hem me in, behind and before,
 and lay your hand upon me.
Such knowledge is too wonderful for me;
 it is so high that I cannot attain it. . . .
For it was you who formed my inward parts,
 you knit me together in my mother's womb.
I praise you, for I am fearfully and wonderfully made.
 Wonderful are your works;
that I know very well.
 My frame was not hidden from you,
when I was being made in secret,
 intricately woven in the depths of the earth.

By now an appropriate sense of awe has settled over the group. Then the initiates are led back into their lives to create masks for themselves, with the help of their community and Creator. To take them back to an earlier time in life, we go to a kindergarten classroom, all set out with supplies for making masks. When their creations are completed, we lead the initiates back to a campfire and invite them to introduce themselves. They speak from within their masks, out of the very center of their identity to the listening world of their fellow initiates.

The masking ritual is a powerful event for these adolescents. It can be particularly helpful as they emerge into early adulthood, when the process of asking questions and getting answers helps them establish their identities. They become a doctor or a plumber or a businessman or a minister or a writer or a musician. Adjectives will be added to give further definition to these selves—a caring doctor, a damn-fine plumber, a savvy businessman, a trusted minister, a struggling writer, a promising musician. Beyond our vocations are more personal aspects of our identity. We also may become a spouse, a parent, a partner, a friend.

We take all these things—and many others—and put them all together to come up with our identity, "a unity of personality now felt by the individual and recognized by others as having a consistency in time," to quote Erikson. We have our individual life structure, "the basic pattern or design of a person's life," to quote Levinson. We have our persona.[3]

HOW MASKS LIMIT GROWTH

Our persona gives us a framework in which to grow. It also limits our growth. In early adulthood we are more aware of its positive aspects. In midlife we become aware of the negative, the limits it places on growth. Those limits will be felt most acutely if either or both of the following conditions pertain to us:

1. If we choose a persona that has great social significance: The more visible and distinctive the role in the greater scheme of things, the more that role will restrict growth.

2. If we fill the role effectively: The more successful one is at being the being one has chosen to be, the more likely one is

to build up a shell that is so restrictive that one must break it, but so thick that one cannot.

I know this story well because it is the story of my own life. In adolescence and early adulthood, I got lots of affirmative answers to the many questions I asked. I became quite successful in constructing an effective persona. I chose to be a minister, which is a role of great social significance, not only to a congregation but also to the wider community. I filled the role well. By the time I was in my early forties I had constructed an admirable identity—an impressive life structure, a fine box—that looked just great from the outside. I had an intelligent, caring, and lovely wife with her own successful career; three handsome, bright, popular, and secure sons; many caring and fine friends; a good job as minister of a substantial church with a strong spiritual program and a commendable social witness. In addition I was the author of a book and leader of workshops and retreats, the owner of two homes and two cars, and the keeper of a cat.

In addition to those visible things were the invisible qualities that I had assumed for myself. I would hear my world tell me, time and again, who I was: talented, creative, supportive and caring, trusted. It was this last word that plagued me the most. "Bill can be trusted," the world said. But at the core of my being, another voice, my own voice, was beginning to scream out the opposite as I remained silent. I won an award as the outstanding citizen in Middletown; the mayor said, "Bill Roberts is the most trusted person . . ." The president of my alma mater (also in Middletown) described me to my classmates at our twenty-fifth reunion as the person who had done more to create a sense of community in this city than anyone else. "People just trust Bill Roberts," he said. Whenever a tragedy happened in town—a suicide or a teenage accident—I was called because "you could trust Bill to say the right thing." Even the homeless trusted me as their spokesperson.

Trust in Bill—what a fine box I had created. It looked great from the outside. But deep inside, I was profoundly unhappy and utterly unable to break out. But I needed the box to keep my sanity—or, at least, my respectability. As the chaos of my midlife journey was tearing me apart, I could still put on my mask, go to work, listen to people, preach a sermon, administer the sacraments, and pretend to know what was happening. And no one seemed to complain.

Later, when I had separated from my wife and family, some strange voice deep within me seemed to complain in a major way. The voice caught my attention through a dream. In this dream I had been charged with some terrible crime and was being detained in a white-tiled room, deep underground. Someone who seemed very nice came to prepare me for my death. He asked me a few questions about what happened. I answered. He then said that there was no reason for me to die because I had obviously been charged unjustly. "You should just file a countersuit," he said. He then led me into the town square, where a judge was seated. Suddenly I protested, "No. That's not fair. My wife is not the reason I am in prison." But then the judge would not release me.

This dream came to me before I began to deal with the first soul task, the breakdown of the persona. I was already deeply involved in the second two—the great encounters with the shadow and the soul mate. In my utter confusion I was blaming everybody but myself for my unhappy condition. And the one I blamed more than any was my wife.

I chanced to share my dream with a friend. She listened deeply and responded with few words. "The dream speaks the truth. Your wife is not the reason you are in prison. Your prison is your job and everything associated with it." She was right. Up until that point in my life, I lived according to my persona orientation. I took the cues for my life from the role I had chosen for myself. Consequently, my role became my prison. When my life became shaky, I held on to my role all the more tenaciously, clinging to the bars of my cell with all my strength. I would not let go until the dream told me I must.

When I dared to leave the familiar surroundings of my own special jail, I was astounded to see how thoroughly my chains not only had held me, but actually had worked their way into the fiber of my being so that I was essentially oblivious to them:

THE PRISONER OF CHILLON

It was at length the same to me
Fettered or fetterless to be,

I learned to love despair.
And thus when they appeared at last,
And all my bonds aside were cast,
These heavy walls to me had grown
A hermitage—and all my own!
And half I felt as they were come
To tear me from a second home:
My very chains and I grew friends,
So much a long communion tends
To make us what we are:—even I
Regained my freedom with a sigh.[4]

I had created such a persona that people in both church and community would not let me abandon it. When I announced that I was leaving the ordained ministry, they refused to believe it. They pleaded. They bargained. They got angry with me. And in some perverse way, I needed it all. I needed them to tell me that I was trusted, because I knew I wasn't worthy of that trust. I needed them to tell me that I was indispensable, because I feared I was worthless. I needed them to keep on believing in that nice fit between Bill Roberts and his shell, because without that shell, I would be nothing. The shell protected me from my own worst fears. It was also keeping me from the rest of my life.

The night when I had that dream and the day when that woman began to redirect my consciousness was the primary crisis point of my midlife passage. It was the moment when, unbeknownst to me, I was making the decision that would affect my future for good or ill. It was the moment when I stopped projecting my shadow stuff onto my wife and began to work on my own stuff. It was the moment when I began the process of turning away from my persona, the creation of which had been the program for the morning of my life, and began to look for a way to converse with the self.

As a result of the decisions I made at that crisis point, I did in fact leave my job, my career, my identity as a trusted and caring and creative and successful minister. Yet to any man who senses that he is now in a similar situation, I would say: *You* do not need to leave your job, your spouse, your children. You do need to change your consciousness from a persona–orientation to the more elusive orientation to the self. You do have to get with the program that is appropriate to the afternoon of your life.

I remember hearing about a chaplain's job at the university, which opened up when I was passing through the most perilous stretch of my midlife journey. I had left the church where I felt comfortable with the value system and honored by the people. I had assumed my position as a senior consultant with the accounting firm, where I was an insignificant novice in a culture that I could not understand and did not respect. I felt an intense craving to go back to my old life as a minister, to "reconstitute my persona," the only one I had ever really known.

When I told my career transition counselor about the opening, he gently nudged me on my way. "Far be it from me to tell you about your mission in life, but I have the feeling you are called to live in different worlds, the practical world of business and the spiritual world where you have been." All I could think at that time was, "Easy for you to say. I'm the one who has to live the life between two worlds, neither fish nor fowl, betwixt and between." As it turned out, I didn't go back. I kept going, pushing the confusion and despair back step by step, until deeper truths began to become clear.

The move from the world of the church to the world of big business required that I put on a new mask. At first that mask did not fit very well and I often wished I could take it off and just be myself, but I had been given a new role and I was obliged to play it. One night, not long after I had been named as the senior vice president of Prudential Residential Services, my role confusion parted for a brief moment and allowed me to see a truth about myself. I had been invited by the president of the company to join her at a summit meeting regarding the future of one of our divisions. We met with executives from Prudential through the day and in the evening sought a place to get a bite to eat. Without knowing it, we found a restaurant which was having, of all things, a convention of psychics. And, again, without realizing what we were doing, we registered for this event as we ordered our meal, and soon discovered that we had won the right to have a psychic consultation.

The consultation began with the request for my watch, which happens to be a Timex costing less than $18. Somewhat derisively, I asked what you could tell from a watch, and this psychic responded instantly, "I can tell that you are a businessman and you have come to New Jersey for a crisis meeting of your company." I resisted her characterization of me as a businessman but immediately heard the voice of our president insisting, "Bill Roberts, you are a business-man. Get used to it!" Her clarity only intensified my confusion, and I soon found myself stammering out an explanation to this psychic. "The fact of the matter is that for twenty-five years I was a clergy-man; it's less than two years that I've been a businessman." "Makes no difference whatsoever," the woman retorted. "You're not a cler-gyman or a businessman. You're a healer and you know it."

I didn't know that then. And I'm not sure I know it now. But I do know that if I had stayed so utterly preoccupied with creating or sustaining either of those social roles—clergyman or business-man—or any other role for that matter—accountant, banker, lawyer, even father—I would not have learned how to listen for the deeper meaning for my life.

LAWS OF NATURE AND HUMAN NATURE

Several concepts from physics and biology have helped me listen for those deeper meanings. One is the second law of thermody-namics, which comes from Newtonian physics. The physicist David Peat explains:

> The second law deals with the direction of change in the universe and dictates that natural processes are always accompanied by an increase in entropy. Since entropy is the measure of the disorder, randomness, and lack of correlation in things, the second law indicates that, left to itself, a system will always run down, fall apart, and decay into disorder and chaos.[5]

This fundamental law of nature is also a law of human nature. Bodies decline and fall apart. Life leads to death and dissolution, generally after a long period known as old age, which is too often a time of disillusion and decay. The reason, from my point of view, is that we try to live the afternoon of our lives according to the pro-gram of the morning. We need a new program for the second half of our lives.

Quantum physics provides us with two fascinating concepts to help us picture what the afternoon's program might look like. The concepts are dissipative structures and autopoiesis.

The first concept, dissipative structures, as the name implies, has to do with the fact that natural structures inevitably weaken, lose energy, and ebb away into nothingness. Yet precisely here is the hope. Ilya Prigogine, the Nobel Prize–winning chemist from the University of Brussels, "discovered that such dissipative activity might play a constructive role in the creation of new structures. Dissipation didn't lead to the demise of the system. It was part of the program by which the system let go of its present form so that it could reemerge in a form better suited to the demands of the present environment."[6]

As things become more complex, along comes something that does not fit the old form. A disturbance, then a fluctuation, and another. The system tries to resist these disturbances, but eventually the new, dissonant information can no longer be ignored. The structures that have held the system together collapse, and chaos takes over.

"But the disintegration does not signal the death of the system," explains Margaret Wheatley. "In most cases the system can configure itself at a higher level of complexity, one better able to deal with the new environment. Dissipative structures demonstrate that *disorder* can be the source of *order*, and that growth is found in disequilibrium, not in balance."[7]

Ilya Prigogine is a chemist; he uses the concept of dissipative structures to describe how reality works at the most fundamental physical level. Margaret Wheatley is not only a professor, but a management consultant; she uses the same concept to describe how companies need to let go of old forms, to risk disequilibrium, disorder, even chaos to fully open to new ways of effectively ordering their systems.

We are considering men at midlife; the same concept of dissipative structures can inform us. Our persona, the structure we have worked so hard to build in the first half of life, must break down, and we must experience the disequilibrium, the disorder, the chaos of midlife, or else the second half of life will be lived according to the program of the second law of thermodynamics. Energy ebbs. Meaning erodes. Men live lives of quiet desperation. And die.

David Whyte promises us something else. David was born in England, lived in Wales, and now resides on an island in Puget Sound, where he writes poetry and consults with Fortune 500 corporations. His concern is helping persons know themselves and stay true to themselves in a workplace that is often seen as dehumanizing. He wrote a poem about a monastery in the Himalayas where exquisitely carved masks express the love of their creator:

THE FACES AT BRAGA

Such love in solid wood!
Taken from the hillsides and carved in silence
they have the vibrant stillness of those who made them. . . .

Carved in devotion
their eyes have softened through age
and their mouths curve through delight of the carver's hand.

If only our own faces
would allow the invisible carver's hand
to bring the deep grain of love to the surface.

If only we knew
as the carver knew, how the flaws
in the wood led his searching chisel to the very core,

we would smile too
and not need faces immobilized
by fear and the weight of things undone. . . .

If only we could give ourselves
to the blows of the carver's hands,
the lines in our faces would be the trace lines of rivers

feeding the sea
where voices meet, praising the features
of the mountain and the cloud and the sky.

Our faces would fall away
until we, growing younger toward death
every day, would gather all our flaws in celebration

to merge with them perfectly,
impossibly, wedded to our essence,
full of silence from the carver's hands.[8]

Part of the challenge of midlife is rediscovering a profound, childlike faith in the universe that the invisible carver is really there and will become reengaged in our life if only we can let go, let the old structure fall away, dissipate, disappear so that the carver can "bring the deep grain of love to the surface." Science tells us that such a faith is reasonable, and the words of the poet David Whyte remind us of one more word from the poetry of the new physics. Erich Jantsch, a systems scientist, has given us the word *autopoiesis*, which is derived from the Greek words meaning "self" and "production." Jantsch summarizes the significance of the word: "It is the characteristic of living systems to continuously renew themselves and regulate this process in such a way that the integrity of their structure is maintained." He then gives us a memorable example. "Caterpillar and butterfly are two temporarily stabilized structures in the coherent evolution of one and the same system."[9]

What if a gorgeous butterfly—say, a monarch or a viceroy—stayed stuck in some earlier state? What if as a larva it refused transformation to its full splendor? Now think how tragic it is when men on the verge of midlife transformation hustle back into the box and reconstitute the old, familiar persona. Think of how valuable it would be if men had a structured way to encourage them to let go of their hard-won masks and invite transformation.

THE FIRST MYSTERY RITE

Our first mystery rite, a midlife variation of the masking ritual for adolescents, provides the needed structure to encourage men to let go of their present state in order to invite creative transformation. This awesome event requires careful preparation.

Over the years I have gathered many groups to start a journey of this type. I recommend that you be intentional and deliberate at this early stage. The design I use most often involves at least a full evening together during which the men can meet one another and get introduced to the issues we bring to the experience. After admittedly perfunctory introductions (most men have been conditioned to introduce themselves in terms of their roles in life, their persona-orientation), we turn to one of the great stories of midlife. These stories can be found in many places. The best collections I know of are by Allan Chinen: *Once Upon a Midlife, In the Ever*

After, and *Beyond the Hero.* I also recommend Clarissa Pinkola Estés, *Women Who Run with the Wolves,* which is not for women only.[10]

Because of my background, I often use stories from the Hebrew Scriptures. Generally, on this first night together we use that terrifying account of Jacob wrestling with a powerful figure at a place called Penuel. I know we will not plumb the depths of this story in the first night, and I fully intend to return to it when we are finally in passage. The story is so archetypally accurate that it allows men to articulate their personal midlife issues.

Whatever story is chosen, it should also help some men decide that they do not want to be part of this group. A deliberate group is one that offers freedom for some to say "no" or "not now." Raise this issue with the group. For those who say "yes," the rite of passage is about to begin with the midlife masking ritual. This serves both as our rite of separation and as our celebration of the breakdown of the persona.

Let me tell you about the first group that I led, beginning with how the ritual was created. After a transition from ministry to business, I finally had a two-week vacation coming. (Corporate people, even corporate officers, get surprisingly little vacation time, especially when compared to their counterparts in church or academia.) As this time approached, I was undecided about going away. Work was busy, my friend Stu was in the midst of his midlife crisis, and I had promised to lead my first rite of passage in less than a month—and I still had not hit upon how the first mystery rite should proceed.

Nevertheless, I traveled across the continent to the shores of Puget Sound. On the second day, while I was still decompressing, the phone rang. I was shocked when I heard, "Stu's dead. He was hit by a car. He's dead."

On the second-to-last day of the vacation, I was walking alone in the British Columbia Museum in Victoria. As I wandered from one exhibit to the next, I came upon one that featured the Kwakiutl people, a Native American tribe that exists to this day in the Pacific Northwest. They are ritualistically mature, and their myths and rites are dramatic and gripping. Their rites of passage are still functional.

As I ambled through the area depicting the initiation to adulthood, I felt as if I were home again. When I saw those masks made by the young men as they assumed their identities within the tribe, I felt as if their essences were coming through those masks into the darkened museum. I was deeply happy.

Then I saw a mask the likes of which I had never seen before—a mask within a mask. And next to it was a mask within a mask within a mask! Blinking—tears were now rolling down my cheeks—I noticed a small sign that directed me to more information. I learned that among the Kwakiutl people all men went through a rite of passage to adulthood. During that rite, they made their masks and were given their identities.[11]

Much later in the life cycle, *some* men were chosen for a second rite of passage. They were allowed to tell the story and sing the songs of Siwidi (or Born-to-Be-Head-of-the-World). Siwidi is one of the legendary figures from primordial time who risked a journey to the undersea kingdom. During this trip he lived in warped time—he thought he was gone for four days but everyone else knew he was away for four years. His goal was to bring back to his tribe the knowledge they would need for life. It was clear that the identity he achieved in early adulthood was not enough. He needed to know the essence of life itself.

Those who are privileged to tell Siwidi's story and sing his dance must make transformation masks to dramatize the various guises that he assumed on his journeys—a mask within a mask (within a mask). The technology of this sacred art form was rather simple. The first mask presented itself. Then, through the use of pulleys, it separated to reveal a deeper reality (and, in some cases, an even deeper level). These deeper realities show forth the essence of the human and the divine. The moment I saw the genius of those so-called primitive Kwakiutl mask makers, I knew I had been given our rite of separation. It could be called the breakdown of the persona, but it also could be called the breakthrough of the self.

Within a month after my walk though that darkened museum, I was leading a group of midlife men, most of whom did not know one another. Fourteen of us gathered on a Tuesday evening to meet one another, to meet Jacob, and to meet that demon Jacob wrestled at Penuel—the same one we were still wrestling that night in Connecticut.

Three nights later, on Friday, twelve of us came back to begin our journey. We gathered and became quiet. I introduced the plans for the evening and invited the others to talk about how they were feeling at this point in the adventure. They seemed ready to proceed, so we read Psalm 139 (Oh Lord, thou has searched me and known me! Thou didst form my inward parts, thou didst knit me together in my mother's womb. Thou knowest me right well; my frame was not hidden from thee when I was being made in secret, intricately wrought in the depths of the earth.) We discussed this ancient wisdom for a short while and prepared to begin our journey together.

When the time seemed right, we went to a room (used by a second-grade Sunday school class) with little tables and little chairs—it felt something like that Wonderland into which Alice had fallen. The tables were covered with stuff from which to make masks: paper bags, crayons, markers, crepe paper, construction paper, doilies, yarn, string, face paint.

The room was ready but the group was not. We felt so awkward. Grown men trying to fit into those little chairs and banging our knees against those child-sized tables. At one point I felt as if the group had been pushed too far, and just as I was about ready to give up on the full ritual and simply discuss what our masks might have looked like, first one man, then another began to play creatively until the entire group was busy at the task of making transformation masks.

Able, successful, respected men—an artist, a lawyer, a banker, three doctors, an architect—were creating masks. Some ran down the hall to the boys' rest room to look at their creations and put on the finishing touches. What a wonderful sight. Men standing in front of little sinks with tiny toilets and urinals behind us, looking in mirrors and seeing strange self-portraits of ourselves as men, masks that would empower personal transformation.

When our masks were ready, we gathered at a campfire (actually candles amidst lava rocks normally used for gas barbecue grills) so we could speak to one another through our creations. Each man put on his mask and spoke about its significance.

The drama we experienced came from the ritual process more than from any artistic creation. The presenting masks, in fact, were remarkably similar, depicting the messages of our everyday lives, strewn with the symbols of work—stethoscopes, paint brushes, pencils in a vest pocket, bow ties. Some contained the names or pictures of children and wives.

Some men had other statements, even on their most exterior of masks. One man was behind bars, like the bars of a prison, while another was all tied up in string. Each made it clear in his description that he could not get himself loose. They tried valiantly, but it was true, evident even on that first night, that they could not free themselves from the bonds of their personae. Neither man had created a mask behind this first mask. Neither was able to reveal anything of his deeper life.

The others in the group did have deeper visages to reveal. Almost always they expressed symbolic playfulness and new life: some were colorful, clownlike, childlike, chaotic; others were somber, for example, one had a big black snake instead of a nose. Two or three probed all the way to the core of the personalities to reveal more gentle signs; one had applied face paint to his own face, transforming himself into an old man full of dignity. The man explained, "I wanted to see what I would look like in old age. I'm not sure I like it. I will decide later."

This sharing took much longer than I had planned. We talked for a long time about who we were and who we were becoming. And then, late at night, we prepared to leave this world of masked men gathered around a campfire by going through a liminal experience. We went to a kitchen and made ice cream sundaes with lots of whipped cream, cherries, chocolate, strawberries, bananas, and nuts. And then we all went home three hours after we had arrived.

Next morning we got a late start. The group had agreed to gather at 9:00 A.M. and stay together for a full day. But at 9:10 A.M. only three men were present; at 9:20 A.M. only six; again I feared that I had pushed too far for a group of modern men, but by 9:30 A.M. the full group had arrived. We gathered and became quiet.

The opening question simply was "How was the night?" Responses were rather immediate. "Awful. I didn't sleep at all." "I couldn't sleep either." And so forth, until one man shared a fuller experience:

I slept but not for a long time. When I came home I left the mask in the car. And then I went back out to get it. Then I left it in the kitchen . . . actually in the basket under the sink. But when I was on the steps I decided to go back and get it. As I was bringing it up the steps, Mary called out, "Tom, are you home?" I carried the mask with me into the bedroom. I regret that I did.

"How was your meeting?" she asked. Good. "What did you do?" she asked. Made a mask. "You're a lot later than I thought you'd be," she said quietly. Sorry, dear.

Somehow, I felt dirty. I felt as if I had done something wrong to Mary.

Imagine, a man experiences a new level of intimacy with himself and he feels dirty. But before I could say a word another man spoke:

I'm sorry I'm late. I almost didn't come. Drove around the block three or four times before I decided to come in. Last night I went home and went into the bathroom to wash off my mask. And I saw my old self in the mirror. At first it scared me. Then I began to think that I really liked it. Just then Pat called, "Are you coming to bed?" I quickly washed off my face. But then I was afraid to tell her. And then when I came here I realized I was afraid to tell you, too. I guess I am in no-man's-land.

And when he said that, I realized that the rite of separation had achieved its purpose. This group of men had crossed the threshold. We were in liminal space. We were betwixt and between. We were over our heads. We were *en passage*. We had embarked on our journey.

We were now ready to meet the first soul brother, Abraham. We were ready to enter into the worship present, the eternal now. A special type of scripture study developed by the East Harlem Protestant Parish in the 1960s provided a four-step method:

1. Read the text in several translations. This not only offers nuances of meaning, but the repetition allows the story to seep in from different angles.

2. Look at unusual or significant words. This involves some preparation by the leader, who needs to preview the text and engage in some research.

3. Close the book and have someone tell, as accurately as possible, what the story actually says.

4. Now ask what the story means for each person—and the meanings are endless.

For nearly thirty years now I have used this discipline with groups—children, adolescents, men, women, men and women. I am frequently astonished by the experience. It's like a movie experience. We all know that a movie is really a lot of snapshots shown in rapid succession, but we completely forget this when we sit in a theater utterly engaged in the drama being played out. In this study method, the stories are really nothing but words on a page. So we read them, word by word, page by page, again and again. Then we look at key words. Then we dare to tell the story without looking at the words on the page. And then we are ready to bring the story to life. We do this by asking questions.

When we start asking the great questions and bringing them to life, we discover that our normal patterns of thought give way to something much more energized. No longer do we think linearly, logically, from question to answer. We begin to think in a more chaotic pattern as the questions jump from side to side, spin and turn, rush forward and back. It's as if primordial time has invaded actual time. The light from long ago begins to shine in the gloom of now.

Our rite of passage is designed so that each of the four soul tasks is shared with a legendary figure who walks with us through a stretch of our midlife wilderness. We generally read the whole story of his life and then go back to focus on a central tale. When we summon a legend to join us on our journey, we fully expect him to walk with us until we are transformed by his presence.

I chose Abraham as our first traveling companion, because he is the best example of someone surviving the breakdown of the persona. We meet him at the moment of his transformation. His name, which has always been *Abram* (simply "Abba," "Father") is about to become *Abraham* ("Father of a Multitude"). But he cannot get to this new being without an incredible act of faith in letting go. (We consider as much of Genesis 12–15 as we can.)

> Now the Lord said to Abram, "Go from your country and your kindred and your father's house to a land that I will show you. And I will make of you a great nation, and I will bless you, and make your name great, so that you will be a blessing." (Genesis 12:1–2)

Let's start the wondering. Wonder what, where, and how Abram heard that voice. Why was he asked to give up everything—"your country and your kindred and your father's house"? Why was he not told where he was going? What did his wife Sarah think? And what about his colleagues and neighbors? Is this man middle-age crazy or what?

And what about me? How do I hear God's voice? What are dreams? What might I be asked to leave behind if I really heard a voice and risked a journey, a faith journey of this sort? Where does one get the courage? How could I ever trust a God who called me on a pilgrimage to "a land that I will show you" and gave no more information than that? Don't we need more assurance? How could I live without a protective shell and wander aimlessly through the desert? What was Abram's first half of life? What did he become in the second? What have I come to be in the first half of my life? And what will I be in the second?

Once the questions start flowing, it is hard to stop them. And they should not be stopped. Do not imagine that they must have answers. Most of the time the questions need to be lived until they present their own answers. Remember life is not a set of problems to be solved, but a mystery to be lived. Brother Abraham is a living mystery from the day he got that call to leave it all behind until the very end. He is the ideal soul brother to give us the faith to let go of our masks and move out into the unknown.

4

THE ENCOUNTER WITH THE SHADOW

One dismal night, Stanley, an old college friend, came to see me. He was in a bad way, out of sorts. He had left his life—wife, family, job, identity. He had pretty much gone through that angry state in which he tried to blame others for this turn of events. Now he was in the lifeless state that precedes new life.

We walked for a long, long time without speaking. The evening grew quiet and dark as the sun faded and the stars shone. Finally, we walked under a street light, and he broke the silence. "See my shadow?" he asked. I could see it resting gently on the fallen leaves. "That's proof that I'm still alive. But it's the only proof I have."

I always knew that Stanley had more courage than most of his peers, but on that night even I was amazed. Most men run from the silence of the shadow. They put all their energies into denying it or spewing it back on others. They rarely look at it and say with Shakespeare, "This thing of darkness I acknowledge mine."

WHAT IS THE SHADOW?

Carl Jung once said, "Everything of substance casts a shadow." Jung met his shadow when he went through that terrifying midlife collapse at the age of thirty-six. As early as 1912 he began using the term. "The shadow side of the psyche" was filled with "not recognized desires" and "repressed portions of the personality." In 1917 he wrote an essay entitled "On the Psychology of the Unconscious," in which he speaks of the personal shadow as *the other* in us, the unconscious personality of the same sex, reprehensible and inferior, that which embarrasses us or shames us. "By shadow I mean the negative side of the personality, the sum of all those unpleasant qualities we like to hide."[1]

Robert Bly talks about the shadow with a wonderful image. He calls it "The Long Bag We Drag Behind Us." In our early years, we had a fully rounded personality—he calls it a 360-degree personality—a ball of energy that radiates from all parts of the psyche. As we grow, we begin to get cues from our parents that some of this energy should not be expressed, that some parts of our psyche are unacceptable. We hear comments like "Can't you be still?" or "It isn't nice to try and kill your brother." In order to keep their parents' love, children respond to these comments by pinching off parts of the personality and stuffing them in the invisible bag. Even before we go to kindergarten, the bag is getting pretty full.

Pretty soon the teachers join the parental chorus. "Good children don't get angry over such little things." Into the bag goes anger. "You colored outside the lines." Into the bag goes our creativity. "Quit acting so cocky!" Into the bag goes our exuberance.

Bly suggests that by the age of twenty, as we emerge into adulthood, that 360-degree personality is reduced to a thin slice, which is all we have available to us when we enter into marriage. "We'll imagine a man who has a thin slice left—the rest is in the bag—and we'll imagine that he meets a woman; let's say they are both twenty-four. She has a thin, elegant slice left. They join each other in a ceremony and this union of two slices is called marriage."[2]

Bly observes that we spend the first twenty years of our life determining what to stuff in our bag, and we spend the rest of our lives trying to get the bag open to retrieve the parts we have lost.

Bly's wonderful description helps explain one aspect of the shadow—the personal shadow. There are other aspects. The family shadow develops as we describe ourselves as a virtuous family, not like those lazy good-for-nothings down the street. There are corporate shadows that are used to hide some of the dismal truths of corporate life. There are aspects of the shadow that come from our profession, our nation, our political affiliation, and, of course, our religion. And, very important, there is the collective shadow, the part of ourselves that derives from our humanity, some of which is just plain evil.

Near the end of the saga of Iron John, Robert Bly tells us how to deal with the shadow. "When a person moves into the black, that process amounts to bringing back all the shadow material, which has been for years projected out there on the faces of bad men and women, communists, witches, and tyrants, back inside. That process could be called retrieving and eating the shadow."[3]

Through much of early adulthood we keep our shadow material out of sight. During that time of life, we are concerned with negotiating an identity, so we develop masks behind which we can hide our depraved stuff. When we discover a part of ourselves that does not jibe with the identity we have developed, we will project it out onto others. My identity tells me I am a nice man; if I get angry, it surely must be because others incite my anger by being so mean, selfish, or insensitive. My mask lets everyone know that I am married, committed to one woman for life; if I feel a desire for a new romance, it surely must be because there is something inadequate about the woman I married. And so it goes for all of the shadow material. In order to keep a consistency of personality, we take any dissonance and project it onto another.

But when we hit midlife, as the mask begins to crack, the shadow is loosed. All that we have successfully projected onto others now needs to be retrieved, brought back into ourselves. Furthermore, it must be fully incorporated into our lives, almost in the way that food is incorporated into our bodies through eating. To understand how this complex process might work, we will consider the three stages of successfully dealing with the shadow—projecting, retrieving, and eating the shadow.

To understand the significance of projection we must remember that we cannot see our own shadow. Precisely because it is unconscious, it is not available for conscious inspection. The psychiatrist R. D. Laing talks about this in a striking way, explaining that until we notice that we fail to notice, we cannot change, because we do not realize how our failure to notice shapes our thoughts and actions.[4]

The shadow remains in our unconscious. It cannot be seen; it can only be observed as it plays itself out on the canvas of something or someone else. This is the process called projection. When some part of us is projected, we see it outside ourselves, as though it belongs to someone else and has nothing to do with us.

"We do not decide to project something, it happens automatically," argues the Jungian analyst John Sanford. "If we decide to project something it would be conscious to us and then, precisely because it is conscious to us, it could not be projected; once something is conscious, projection ceases."[5]

Projection is not necessarily a bad thing. Indeed, one could argue, recognizing our projections is a crucial stage in knowing ourselves. In a courageously conscious way, my friend Stanley, who felt utterly lifeless, was groping for ways to know that he was still himself and a person of value; when he saw his shadow on the ground, he knew that he was still alive, and that was the first step in his recovery. Once he saw the shadow and knew that it really did come from him, not someone else, he could actually study the shadow to get some glimpse of the shape of the self.

Once we start knowing our projections and use them not to blame or hurt another but to know ourselves, we can begin the process of retrieving the shadow, bringing it back into ourselves. Derek Walcott, the Jamaican poet who won a Nobel Prize in 1992, wrote a poem about welcoming the rejected parts of the self:

LOVE AFTER LOVE

The time will come
when, with elation,
you will greet yourself arriving
at your own door, in your own mirror,
and each will smile at the other's welcome,

and say, sit here. Eat.
You will love again the stranger who was your self.
Give wine. Give bread. Give back your heart
to itself, to the stranger who has loved you

all your life, whom you ignored
for another, who knows you by heart.
Take down the love letters from the bookshelf,

the photographs, the desperate notes,
peel your own image from the mirror.
Sit, feast on your life.[6]

What a wonderful thing to invite your rejected parts back into your life. To sit with them. To love again the stranger who was yourself. To feast on your life. To not only retrieve the shadow, but eat it, chewing it up, swallowing it, and then, miraculously, being transformed by its life–giving energy. But it is not as easy as it might seem.

NEARLY CHOKING ON MY OWN SHADOW

When I was in the depths of my despair, I met a part of my shadow and tried to retrieve and eat it—and I nearly gagged. Only much later was I able to digest the meaning of the experience. It happened on a holiday, an awful, lonely time for those who are alone but do not wish to be.

When I could not stand the loneliness any longer, I called a friend and asked if I might come by. I had depended on this friend through so much melancholy that I sensed that I had become a pest. But his spouse encouraged him, and he suggested some time later that afternoon. I went—we walked and he talked. He had heard enough of my sad story that he really did not want to hear any more, and so my friend, who happens to be a psychotherapist, tried to humor me. "We have to paint lines on our parking lot down at the office. We've noticed that our patients are parking according to their diagnoses. Schizophrenics take up two spaces. Obsessives park so close to the next car they can't open the door. Paranoids always back in."

As he continued to talk, I dared to ask, "What is my diagnosis?" "You don't want to know," he said. "No, I really do want to know." "Not now," he responded, smiling wryly. "C'mon, you're supposed to be my friend. Tell me the truth." "Okay," he said with a slight pause, "You're narcissistic."

I asked what that meant—what that meant for me. "Well, narcissists spend their lives trying to get people to mirror back approval. They will do anything to get approval, even adoration. The good ones actually construct whole environments that will feed them approval." (Suddenly, I thought of my relationship with the congregation.) "Narcissists," he continued, "have thousands of tentacles that can pick up signals from their worlds. On each tentacle, thousands of sensors. And all these sensors are constantly working to pick up signs of approval." I took all of this in.

"What do you do to cure narcissism?" I asked. "It's a character disorder," he responded grimly. "I don't think you can finally cure it. It comes from a wound, probably very early in life. You just have to know that you have that wound. Become conscious of how you try to fill the wound with mirrored approval. You tend to vacillate between being grandiose and being depressed. You're always afraid of being humiliated, so you always have to make sure you're smart, respected, powerful, sexy. It's a helluva way to live and can be miserable for those who try to live with you. The challenge is to learn to live on the edge of the wound rather than going into it all the time. Oh, by the way, I know about this because we share this diagnosis. I'm a narcissist, too." (Today, my friend and I look back on this conversation and smile, for we are the founding fathers of our own twelve-step program called NA—Narcissists Anonymous. But on that day I was not smiling. I was demanding.)

"So if you're a narcissist, what did you do about it?" "Well, I heard this psychotherapist speak. He was apparently known as a specialist in narcissism. He said a few things that cut right to the core of me. He was very helpful. Made all the difference in the world."

At this point I was desperate, and since my own therapist was trekking in the Swiss Alps, I called this psychiatrist, made an appointment, drove to the library to check out books on narcissism, and began what I assumed would be a lifelong struggle to understand this aspect of my nature.

To be honest, my time with that counselor was not generally helpful. I think he practiced what I would call "adjustment therapy"—see yourself as a victim of some early childhood wound and try to be as normal as you can, given the sad fact of this wound. Furthermore, he was certain that I would need years of therapy with him in order "to reconstruct the objects associated with this early wound." When my personal therapist returned from the Alps and heard my story, his response initially seemed dismissive. "Of course you're narcissistic. The issue is not whether you are this or that diagnosis. The issue is what you do with your self-knowledge. The issue is transformation. Now about that . . ." And with that comment, the hard work of retrieving and eating the shadow of my narcissism was truly and surely begun.[7]

That night I had a dream. There were bears. Lots of bears. Big, powerful black bears. And a few rather feeble white bears. The black bears could clobber the white bears, and they seemed to take sadistic pleasure in doing just that. Finally, because they were exhausted and it was winter, all the bears lay down to sleep. When they woke up they were Pandas.

The next morning I woke up different. No longer so afraid of my inadequacies, my shadow, even my narcissism, I could open my eyes to life in a new way. I could even think about my wounds in a new way.

Ever since I was a little boy, every time I got hurt, there was some voice telling me to disregard my wounds. "You'll be okay. Get up and shake it off. Be tough. Be a man." I learned my lessons well. When I was in high school, I wrestled with a broken rib. I ran the 100-yard dash and then the 220 with shin splints. I pole-vaulted, maybe even in that same track meet, and hurt myself when I landed. I limped on that leg for three weeks, until I had two more falls and had to be carried to a doctor. It turned out I had broken my pelvic bone. Several weeks later, as my pelvis was healing, the X rays showed that I had developed a slipped femur epiphysis. I couldn't hide this wound from the world. I was on crutches for two years and had to wear an orthopedic shoe with a two-inch lift.

Even then I didn't unlearn my boyhood lesson. During my college years I broke up a double play with my nose, but managed to run to third base—safely—before they helped me off the field and to the hospital, where the surgeons ground the bones of my face back into place—pretty much back into place.

But I *still* didn't leave the macho way I had learned so well! When I was in graduate school—theological seminary, no less—I played rugby. Once, early in a game, I got kicked in the hand— hard. I "shook it off," as I had been trained to do, even though my little finger dangled helplessly at the end of my left hand. Reasoning that the team could not possibly win without a scrum half— rugby permits no substitutions, even for injuries—I played the game to the end, to the great admiration (or so it seemed) of my teammates.

That night I had a date for a postgame party. I tried to get to the hospital to get the finger X-rayed, but there wasn't enough time between the game and the party. Anyway, I thought, my date would surely be impressed. To my surprise, she was not. My date for that party is now my wife, and she is still dismayed when she looks at that crooked finger I once tried to wear as a badge of courage.

At midlife we men are invited to stop the charade. Visit our wounds, not only the physical ones but also the psychological and spiritual ones. Learn from them. David Whyte helped me understand what this meant. "Our wounds help us to know what is missing in our lives." Whyte loves the word *bliss*, which comes from *blissaire*, French for "wound." "We see wounds as scars, flaws, blemishes, but they are really our plumage, our peacock feathers." Our wounds are the places were the self is open to the world.

Our wounds are the distinctive marks on our souls. Only by knowing them can we know our unique selves. Only by going through the deep cave to which we have banished all of our wounds can we hope to see the light of the new day. Erich Neumann, a Jungian analyst, presents this fundamental truth this way: "The Self lies hidden in the Shadow; he is the keeper of the gate, the guardian of the threshold. The way to the Self lies through him; behind the dark aspect that he represents there stands the aspect of wholeness, and only by making friends with the Shadow do we gain the friendship of the Self."[8]

JACOB AS SOUL BROTHER

What we need at this point in our lives is a masculine model who isn't afraid of his wounds. Jacob, who is our soul brother as we travel through the shadowland, is just the man. He went to a place called Penuel. There he was wounded and transformed. Lamed and renamed:

> That same night he arose and took his two wives, his two maids, and his eleven children and crossed the ford of the Jabbok. He took them and sent them across the stream, and likewise everything that he had. And Jacob was left alone and a man wrestled with him until the breaking of the day.
>
> When the man saw that he did not prevail against Jacob, he touched the hollow of his thigh: and Jacob's

thigh was put out of joint as he wrestled with him. Then he said, "Let me go for the day is breaking." But Jacob said, "I will not let you go, unless you bless me." And he said to him, "What is your name?" And he said, "Jacob." Then he said, "Your name shall no more be called Jacob, but Israel, for you have striven with God and with men, and have prevailed." Then Jacob asked him, "Tell me, I pray, your name." But he said, "Why is it that you ask my name?" And there he blessed him. So Jacob called the name of the place Penuel, saying, "For I have seen God face to face, and yet my life is preserved." The sun rose upon him as he passed Penuel, limping because of his thigh. (Genesis 32:22–31)

Jacob is our traveling companion for this part of the journey. He is a bona fide scoundrel. Tricked his brother Esau into giving him the birthright (Genesis 25:29–34), scandalously duped his father into giving him a blessing (27:1–45), cheated his father-in-law out of all the good sheep (30:25–36), and most important, all through the first half of his life, deceived *himself* and shaped an identity around that non-name, Jacob—the Usurper, the Trickster, the Devious One.

Only at Penuel, that despairing night of the soul, when Jacob wrestled with whatever—a man, a god, an angel, a devil, the demon whatever—only then was Jacob broken so that Israel could come to life. "Your name shall no more be called Jacob, but Israel, for you have striven with God and with men, and have prevailed" (32:28).

Let's go to Penuel, enter through the eternal now, and wonder about our brother Jacob . . . and, of course, ourselves. Why did he leave his two wives, and two maids, and eleven children on one side of the Jabbok? What happened when he stepped into the stream, his soul's river, and then stepped out into that other world? Surely this is at the threshold of the senses. Can we know that level of the unconscious consciously?

What is this shadowy figure who met him that night? Human? God? God-Human? A power? A demon? A personal dynamism?

Why can't we see the face? And what would we see *if we could* see the face? What are our deepest fears about that face? No, the *deepest* ones! Is there any hope for us if we see the face? And are seen face to face?

What about that wound? A broken hip, it says. A lifelong limp. He's an invalid! In–valid! Not valid!

And the name change? How does Jacob become Israel? How do any of us Devious Men ever get a new name? Can we possibly see God face to face, with all God's knowing of our evil underside, and still have our lives preserved?

Remember there are no answers to these questions. Just mysteries.

THE RITE OF ENCOUNTERING THE SHADOW

That dark night at Penuel obscures much mystery. But this mystery is so central to our quest that we have designed a rite to take us to our Penuel. The rite might be called a liturgical dance. We have called it Crossing the Soul's River. It begins with a period of preparation. We tell the old story of Jacob's wrestling with the demon. We talk about the forces that keep men from tending to their wounds, that block us from recognizing that in forming our identities we, like Jacob, have become deceptive and, in key ways, don't know ourselves fully. Then we cover ourselves with ashes so that we will be invisible in the darkness. Like Jacob, we leave behind everything we have—wives, children, possessions—and approach the river's edge. At that point, one of us, on behalf of all of us, steps into the water and heads off into the shadows of the other side, where he meets a mysterious force that challenges him to grapple for his life.

That wrestling match, even though in some ways it is just a liturgical dance, becomes a battle between life and death—a life that is informed with courageous self-knowledge as compared to what so many live: lives of quiet desperation, which are little better than death. The wrestler knows he can be pinned, not simply defeated but utterly humiliated. He also knows that if he can stay in the struggle, not only will he benefit from his efforts, but his brothers will also.

There are several predictable and terrifying moments in the drama. One occurs when the force touches the hollow of the thigh and the protagonist is deeply wounded. At that moment, all men go to their own wounds and tend to them in a new way. Robert Bly has men put strips of red cloth on their wounds. He says that soon the place fills up like a Red Sea waiting to be parted as God's fierce wind blows over it (see Genesis 14:10–29). The strips of red cloth help us know where to find the painful places.

It is important to visit these wounds, for we need the wisdom of our wounds to speak to us. Men are conditioned to be strong, to deny our hurts, and, therefore, we never learn their meanings—not even of the hurts we inflict upon ourselves. We stay with our wounds as long as we need to, but we must remember that we are called to visit our wounds, not to take up residence there.

For eventually, the day will dawn on this wrestling match. The old story tells us that Jacob had fought so valiantly that his adversary begged to be released from the battle. "Let me go for the day is breaking." But by now Jacob knows that there is a blessing to be had from this struggle. And so he demands his due. "I will not let you go unless you bless me." And with that he is given a new name. He is no longer Jacob, he is now Israel—one who struggles with God.

The final moment in this drama occurs when our brother limps back across the river and tells us that he is a changed man. And assures each of us that we can be also.

The walk back from the river is a time to cool down. It is hot at Penuel. Hot as hell. And moist and damp and full of potential for new life. But we still have to come back from that liminal space and time, to see the wives and children that we left behind.

5

THE ENCOUNTER WITH THE SOUL MATE

No issue causes more grief—or conflict—between women and men than the encounter with the soul mate. Many men know only this part of the midlife passage. Somehow the dreamy soul mate gets activated within their souls, and they project the negative aspects of the feminine onto their spouse and the positive aspects onto another woman. Both women are bruised by the confusion that surrounds this encounter.

Without having any idea what's going on inside him, the man solves his current dilemma by divorcing one and marrying (or moving in with) the other. So common is this at midlife that most people think it is the whole story. Talk shows dedicate hours to "Surviving Your Husband's Midlife Crisis," and everyone seems to know that they are really talking about his midlife affair. The situation, however, is not as simple as this, and it need not be as damaging as such shows report.

WHAT IS THE SOUL MATE?

In Jungian psychology the term for "soul mate" is *anima* (the feminine form) or *animus* (the masculine form), which comes from Latin and means "soul." A man's soul mate is his anima; a woman's, her animus. Closely related is the Latin word *animare*, which means "to animate," "to enliven," "to bring to life." The terms are ambiguous, and in writing about them it is necessary to respect the ambiguity. "Anima and animus remain somewhat borderline concepts, verifiable in experience, useful in therapy, practical when we apply them to ourselves, but at the same time not capable of being precisely defined."[1]

It seems that a particular notion of the feminine is somehow preconfigured in our unconscious. No one knows where this notion comes from. Perhaps, says Bly, it's "some template in our genetic memory."[2] A man can know his anima is activated when he sees a woman (I call her the "anima approximate") who unconsciously fits the template, and he suddenly becomes different and hears phrases coming out of his mouth like "I feel as if I've known her all my life" or "If I were a woman she's what I'd be like" or "If only I could hold her, I would have all that energy within me" or simply "She's perfect." But maybe the man doesn't say anything, but discovers more spring in his walk, more energy in his life, more volume in his laugh, more of a desire to be in those places she's likely to be.

Very often, in an effort to get more clarity about this experience of the soul mate, the question will be asked, "But is the anima a flesh and blood woman or is it just some figment of the imagination?" The answer, even to this pointed question, must remain vague. Indeed, to give additional appreciation for the confusion surrounding this concept, two writers offer powerful but conflicting images in their explanations of how the anima is experienced. Gail Sheehy introduces the modern "Testimonial Woman." John Sanford describes the more ancient "Shaman Wife."

Sheehy explains the meaning of the word *testimonial*. The root of the word is *testis* (plural *testes*). "I read somewhere that when one aboriginal man bumped into another he cupped the sexual parts of his tribesman in greeting. It was 'a testimonial to his manhood.'"[3] The Testimonial Woman offers this same service to her man—she fortifies his masculinity.

Sanford's study of the primitive shaman discovered that the man frequently had a tutelary spirit who assisted him in his work and instructed him in the healing arts. She acted as a spirit wife to him. She assured him, "I love you. I have no husband now; you will be my husband and I shall be a wife unto you. I shall give you assistant spirits. You are to heal with their aid, and I shall teach and help you myself."[4] Whereas the Testimonial Woman does little more than fortify her man's masculinity, the Shaman Wife makes her man whole so he can be the healer he is called to be.

Keeping in mind the perplexity that accompanies the concept of the anima, there are other, more practical questions that demand our attention. For instance, why does the anima get so animated when men are at midlife? Bly suggests that men do not have enough consciousness before then to be affected by the encounter. Of course, men throughout their lives have encountered females—as a mother at birth and in early development, as teachers in school, as classmates, and even as girlfriends. We meet the erotic feminine many times when we are growing up, but Bly ignores them all for, "though sweet, they are not 'it.' The relatively unconscious man at twenty–four may have an affair with a relatively unconscious woman who is twenty-four and nothing happens. . . . Usually both have less consciousness after the affair than they had before."[5]

But at midlife all that stuff about femininity that was pushed into the unconscious begins to emerge as the anima becomes more active. Deep within us a transformation is occurring. The anima, which we have known primarily as a mother figure since infancy, is beginning to take a much more enticing shape, causing us great confusion. That confusion causes many men in midlife to question the merit of their marriage. And that reassessment is most often a life–wrenching experience.

This calls forth a very practical question: What is the relationship of the anima and the love she seems to inspire to marriage? Robert Johnson, in *We: Understanding the Psychology of Romantic Love*, provides a helpful distinction between the finite and the infinite: "When a man tries to live his soul within a *finite* marriage, . . . his soul keeps trying to pull the relationship toward the *infinite*, make it into an allegory of love, death, and paradise lost, convert this human marriage into a huge, sweeping, archetypal drama. The drama goes on inside him, anyway, all the time—at the fantasy level. If he could learn to keep it there, to see it as symbol, then he could live correctly with his soul."[6]

When we ask our wives to join our cosmic drama, we are always disappointed because our wives must live their own dramas, not play a supporting role in ours. And in that disappointment with our wives we often reach out to the anima-approximate, who, especially if she is younger and has not reached a level of psychological maturity, may well become our Testimonial Woman and accept a supporting role in our drama.

It would be my hope for men who divorce at midlife and re-marry that they would learn to differentiate those two worlds—the *finite* and the *infinite*—and not allow their new partners to accept supporting roles. It would be my hope for those who stay married that they would know the agony and the ecstasy of the *finite* relationship of marriage, to use this committed relationship as "a soteriological pathway." (Soteriology is the study of salvation. When viewed in psychological terms, salvation is about individuation or fulfillment.)

This unusual and dramatic description of marriage comes from a Swiss psychotherapist named Adolf Guggenbuhl-Craig. He argues that the lifelong dialectical encounter between two partners, the bond of man and woman until death, creates a way for discovering the soul: "Only through rubbing oneself sore and losing oneself is one able to learn about oneself, God, and the world. For those who are gifted for the soteriological pathway of marriage, it, like every such pathway, naturally offers not only trouble, work, and suffering, but the deepest kind of existential satisfaction. Dante did not get to Heaven without traversing Hell."[7]

Dante's experience with the anima, by the way, can be instructive for us, for he was a man who could keep his loves—the finite and the infinite—separate in his own mind. His masterpiece, *The Divine Comedy*, begins with these words about midlife:

> In the middle of the road of my life
> I awoke in a dark wood
> Where the true way was wholly lost.

During this dismal and confusing time in his life, Dante was sustained by a most unusual woman named Beatrice, whom he had met when they were both children. At the age of nine Dante saw and instantly fell in love with Beatrice, a case of love at first sight. (It is important to note that when a person "falls in love," and especially in cases of "love at first sight," projection is involved. How could there be any other explanation for loving someone who is essentially unknown? But just because it is projection does not mean that it is not real.) This is Dante's description of his nine-year old love: "Her dress on that day was a most noble color, a subdued and goodly crimson, girdled and adorned in such sort as suited with her very tender age. At that moment I say most truly that the spirit of life, which hath its dwelling in the secretest chamber of the heart, began to tremble so violently that the least pulses of my body shook therewith."

Nine years later, when Dante was eighteen, he saw her again and was again overwhelmed. "It happened that the same wonderful lady appeared to me dressed all in pure white. Passing through a street, she turned her eyes thither where I stood sorely abashed (and) saluted me with so virtuous a bearing that I seemed then and there to behold the very limits of blessedness. I parted thence as one intoxicated."[8]

That was the last time he actually saw Beatrice. At age twenty-three she married someone else and died shortly thereafter. Dante also married someone else, but Beatrice was with him all through his life, and especially at midlife. When he was lost in the wilderness, Beatrice reappeared and offered to guide him to Paradise.

MY ENCOUNTER WITH THE SOUL MATE

My encounter with my anima took its first steps forward in a small, barren cell in a Jesuit spiritual center in Pennsylvania. I was then in my mid-thirties and had been given a grant to study "Spirituality in a Protestant Context." On the day after Easter, I left my family and congregation to begin eight days of silence in the spiritual exercises of Ignatius Loyola. Each day, three times a day, I would pray the hours—an hour of preparation, an hour of meditation, and an hour of reflection. On the first several days those prayer times felt like an eternity, but as the days passed and I became more comfortable with what I called "the pyrotechnics of the unconscious," the hours passed like minutes.

On perhaps the seventh day I was to meditate on a passage from Paul's letter to the Philippians: "Rejoice in the Lord always; again I say rejoice. . . . And the peace of God, which passes all understanding will keep your heart and mind in Christ Jesus" (4:4, 7). I began my preparation at my desk in the corner of this barren cell that had become my world. But something invited me to lie down on the floor. And something changed the floor into a green pasture—a lush green pasture in the midst of a wooded glen, beside a stream that bubbled along ever so quietly. Gentle, still waters.

And then something—no, someone—came to me. And caressed me. And anointed not only my head, but every part of my body, my being—loved me and entered me. And I moved this way and that and it felt nice. And my soul was restored. And she spoke, "Just say 'peace.' Just feel peace. No other word. No other thought. Just relaxed. Easy. Peace." And she left quietly.

Within a matter of hours my wise old Jesuit guide came to my cell. I quickly told him, as best I could, what had happened. He smiled, I think, a slight smile. And gave me a poem from Hugh of Saint Victor, a twelfth-century mystic:

What is that sweet thing
that comes sometimes to touch me
at the thought of God?

It affects me with such vehemence and sweetness
that I begin wholly to go out of myself
and to be lifted up, whither I know not.
My consciousness rejoices.

I love the memory of my former trials,
my soul rejoices,
my mind becomes clearer,
my heart is enflamed,
my desires are satisfied.

I feel myself transported to a new place,
I know not where.
I grasp something interiorly
as with the embrace of love.

I do not know what it is,
and yet I strive with all my strength to hold it
and not to lose it.

I struggle deliciously to prevent myself
leaving this thing which I desire to embrace forever,
and I exult with ineffable intensity,
as if I had at last found the goal of my desires.

I seek for nothing more.
I wish for nothing more.

All my aspiration is to continue
at the point that I have reached.

Is it my Beloved?
Yes, it is truly thy Beloved who visits thee. . . .

Therefore, in the times of his absence
thou shalt console thyself;
and during his visits
thou shalt renew thy courage.[9]

For years I held that vision close to my heart without sharing it with another soul. I did console myself in times of her absence and I did, I confess, hope beyond hope that somehow this mysterious Beloved would take human form and visit me again. And that hope continued to grow until I had constructed an elaborate cosmic drama that had to do with the feminine figure I met in the monastery.

In this drama I was fully prepared to project all the negative characteristics onto some woman and all the positive ones onto another. My wife was cast by me in the negative role, but she refused to accept it. I held auditions for women to play the positive role, but no one was willing to assume that role either. Because no woman would accept these supporting roles in the drama I had constructed within my head, I was forced to retrieve all my yearnings, take them back into myself, and focus on the inner struggle in my soul. In doing so I began to understand how the soul mate develops over the course of a lifetime.

ANIMA DEVELOPMENT — THE FOUR STAGES OF THE SOUL MATE

Years ago, I read a brief description of anima development.[10] This particular explanation used four feminine figures to show the progression. First is Eve, the mother of all humans. Then comes Helen, that beautiful woman whose face launched a thousand ships. Next is Mary, the spiritual companion. Last comes Sophia, wisdom herself. Long forgotten until I entered midlife and met my soul mate in that monastery, I began to appreciate the significance of these four figures within my own life.

As a grown man, I was ready to grow beyond Eve. My own mother had been dead for almost two decades. My wife, the mother of my children, was pursuing her own career. In this vacuum a Helen figure presented herself. Soon these two feminine figures, Eve and Helen, were joined in a great battle within my soul. It's hard to explain what this battle was like. I have two vivid memories that might help with the explanation. One day, shortly before my wife and I separated for the first time, we were at our family vacation home. She was playing with our children in the living room, filling the mother role as she did so ably. I was in the kitchen preparing supper, when suddenly I was visited by another woman. She seemed real. I could smell her perfume, feel her touch, delight in her presence.

This experience was confusing to say the least. A few days later, when I told my therapist about this strange experience, he did not seem alarmed; in fact, he had almost predicted this would happen. "There are two women battling within your soul," he said. To repeat: No real flesh and blood women were engaged in this battle. All the women I might have called to this cosmic drama were already about the task of living their own lives. They were not the least bit interested in what was going on inside me as I prepared supper in the kitchen.

What was happening, I now believe, is that the anima was transforming herself. Since I was an infant, my image of femininity was tied up with mother, not just my mother, but Mother. The woman I married became not only the mother of my children, but in some ways the bearer of my infantile notions. Of course, I experienced her as caring for me, like the good mother. I also experienced her as controlling me, like the not-so-good mother.

A second memory from our vacation home: After my wife and I separated, I moved from our house to a friend's spare bedroom, to an apartment, to a borrowed home, to a condo. During this time I really had no home for which to care—no lawn to mow, no leaves to rake, no walks to shovel, no improvement projects to undertake. I was surprised at how much I missed all those domestic tasks.

So I decided to paint the interior of our home on Cape Cod. It was a long weekend and it was a big job. As I became more fatigued, I began to make mistakes. The brush filled with white paint would just go up on the dark wood and leave an unsightly white mark. Then I heard my wife's voice: "Bill, be careful." The next time the brush went out on its own, the voice was even stronger: "Can't you watch what you're doing!" Through the late afternoon, this process accelerated. The brush went out of control. The voice tried all the harder to control me.

At one point in my exhaustion and confusion, I simply stopped painting, looked around at this empty house, and came to realize that the voice was neither my wife's nor my mother's. It was Eve, the mother within me, the one that I knew so well since before birth and that was still, at that midlife moment, the dominant notion of femininity in my soul. But she was changing, even as I painted.

Men at midlife frequently have children who are in the midst of adolescence. The term comes from the French word *adolescere*, which means "to grow up." The word *adult* comes from the same root—*adolescent* from the present participle (one growing up); *adult* from the past participle (one grown up). But the word is deceiving, for as adults we are not finished growing up just because we have left our parents' homes and created our own. We are still growing all through life, and especially at that point when our children launch out on their own and our spouse can now let her role as mother evolve. As the children leave she has less to *do* as a mother. Or to say it another way, she doesn't need to *be* a mother in the way she did when the children were young.

In part because of these changes outside us, we are at that point of psychological development when, deep within us, the anima is ready to transform herself. And one of the great opportunities for growth occurs when we dare to turn to the mother figure in our souls and invite her transformation. The transformation is complex and confusing. No wonder so many men cast about during midlife. No wonder so many men reject the woman who has been the mother of their children, the one who often embodies the earliest stage of anima development—Eve, the mother of all humanity. No wonder so many men seek out Helen, that idealized and glittering woman whose face inspires men to conquer new worlds. No wonder so much pain and hurt and grief gets inflicted by midlife men on their women—and themselves.

When we men can distinguish between the infinite and the finite feminine, then anima development—the development of the feminine within our souls—can move beyond the crisis point of getting stuck on Helen, the beloved. We need to meet Mary, our spiritual companion, and finally to behold Sophia, wisdom herself.

The importance of this development can be seen in such issues as power and control. When my anima was Eve (mother), she had all the power and I had to control myself, be a good little boy, to protect myself from being overwhelmed by her power. With gorgeous Helen, I was out of control, falling desperately in love but always fearing that I might someday be found lacking, powerless, impotent.

With Mary, the spiritual companion, power and control recede as issues, indeed, they become almost like a good conversation on a long hike—one talks, the other listens; then the first listens and the other talks; or one leads, the other follows; then the second leads and the first follows. With Sophia, both power and control dissolve as we find ourselves drawn to an inner logic or logos that seems to have been with us from the beginning. The feminine figure becomes a muse for us, gently empowering us to become the poet of our own lives, autopoiesis.

I will be forever grateful to the women of my life for teaching me about the Inner Woman of the Soul, the soul mate. I believe that they gave me the opportunity and maybe even the obligation to share the insights with other men.

AN EXERCISE FOR ENCOUNTERING THE SOUL MATE

In my work with groups of men—be they within religious communities or in corporate settings—I frequently use an exercise for uncovering the genetic templates of masculinity and femininity hidden in our unconscious.[11] A rather simple technique helps us get hints about our anima by identifying anima–approximates. It also makes us conscious of our emotions and reactions when the anima is activated.

Take a piece of paper and write the names of a number of women—maybe ten or twelve—to whom you are attracted. Identify the traits—physical and personal—that make each woman attractive. Review your list, looking for traits that are common among your attractions. Guess what your set of attractive traits might have been five or ten years ago. How are your patterns of attraction changing? Finally, try to become conscious of how you respond when you find yourself attracted—and attractive—to these women. Do you become uneasy? Do you push them away? Or do you seek to draw them to you?

I am generally amazed at the response to this simple exercise. Men who rarely have the opportunity to think about their relationship with the feminine become aware of different notions of feminine attractiveness and of how those notions change as we mature. Often men come close to talking in terms that suggest healthy anima development. They seem to be moving from Eve to Helen to Mary to Sophia. They often reflect amazing sensitivity to the transition times—the moments when Eve evolves to Helen, Helen to Mary, and Mary to Wisdom Herself.

Exploring the Transition to Helen

To help men understand these transitions, I frequently rely on women writers who have created some of the most convincing characters. Toni Morrison offers us two of them. In her novel *Jazz* she tells of a man named Joe who is married to Violet. Joe sells sundries to women, who are instinctively drawn to him, gathering around him and doing the things women, especially mothers, do— "flicked lint off my jacket, pressed on the shoulder to make me sit down. It's a way they have of mending you, fixing what they think needs repair."

But one woman is different. "She didn't give me a look or say anything. But I knew where she was standing and how, every minute. She leaned her hip on the back of a chair in the parlour, while the women streamed out of the dining room to mend me and joke me. Then somebody called out her name. Dorcas. I didn't hear much else."

Joe tries to explain what it is about Dorcas that is so special, but he simply cannot. "I never got too close to anybody. . . . I couldn't talk to anybody but Dorcas and I told her things I hadn't told myself. With her I was fresh, new again."[12] My question to men who are struggling to describe their Helen is, What made Dorcas so special for Joe? The answers run the gamut, although most of them focus on Dorcas's uncanny ability to make Joe feel like a man, a grown-up man.

Exploring the Transition to Mary

For men who are further in their journey, who are prepared to see women fundamentally as companions, I find myself moving away from the biblical Mary, mother of Jesus, because she has been so sanitized by the church. Indeed it is another character from Toni Morrison who seems to maintain the purity associated with Mary but adds a certain zesty mystery that captures what many men are looking for in a feminine companion.

In the novel *Beloved* we are introduced to the Thirty-Mile Woman. We never actually meet this woman, who is a slave named Patsy. We know her through a remarkable man named Sixo. "Sixo went among the trees at night. For dancing. To keep his blood lines open, he said. Privately, alone he did it." Even though those trees were like brothers to him—in fact, his favorite was called Brother— the deepest parts of his being could be brought to life only by Patsy.[13]

> Once he plotted down to the minute a thirty-mile trip to see a woman. He left on a Saturday when the moon was in the place he wanted it to be, arrived at her cabin before church on Sunday and had just enough time to say good morning before he had to start back again so he'd make the field call on Monday morning. He had walked for seventeen hours, sat down for one, turned around and walked seventeen more. Halle and the Pauls spent the whole day covering Sixo's fatigue from Mr. Garner. Sprawled near Brother, his flame red tongue hidden from them, his indigo face closed, Sixo slept through dinner like a corpse. Now *there* was a man and that was a *tree*.[14]

I have shared Sixo's journey with groups of men, asking them to imagine what the Thirty-Mile Woman *did* for Sixo. Rarely do the men talk about sex, especially in the limited sense of sexual activity or sexual intercourse. Most often they talk about her changing him in far more profound ways. "But how would she do that?" I will ask. One man answered, "She'd listen and listen and listen. She'd hear all about his broken-up parts. And then when she spoke, she would give him back himself whole."

Male yearning for intimacy at midlife is fundamentally about this connection and reconnection, not about a romp in the hay. It is about being with another who listens and hears all about our wounds, and, when she speaks, we find ourselves whole. She listens to the innermost secrets of our hearts, often our broken hearts. Then she reflects them back to us in such a way that our being is enhanced.

Exploring the Transition to Sophia

The final stage in anima development is represented by Sophia, whose name in Greek means "wisdom." This figure appears in the Hebrew Scriptures time and again. Indeed, one whole group of writings is called the Wisdom Literature. The book of Proverbs gives an elaborate description of Sophia. She speaks directly to us:

> Ages ago I was set up,
> > at the first, before the beginning of the earth.
> When there were no depths, I was brought forth
> > when there were no springs abounding with water.
> Before the mountains had been shaped
> > Before the hills, I was brought forth;
> before God made the earth with its fields
> > or the first of the dust of the world.
>
> When God established the heavens, I was there,
> > when God drew a circle on the face of the deep,
> when God made firm the skies above,
> > when God established the fountains of the deep,
> when God assigned the sea its limit,
> > so that the waters might not transgress God's command,
> when God marked out the foundations of the earth
> > then I was beside God, like a master workman
> and I was daily God's delight,
> > rejoicing in God's inhabited world
> and delighting in the sons of men. (Proverbs 8:24–31 alt.)

Sophia, feminine wisdom, has been with us for a long time—indeed, from before time. But she has been pushed into the background, out of consciousness by centuries of patriarchy (in our cultural life) and decades of making a name for ourselves (in our personal lives).

As we move through midlife—generally, by the way, after the confusion that surrounds the transformation of the anima from Eve to Helen—and after we have experienced meaningful feminine companionship, we begin to discover feminine wisdom. This wisdom comes to us at many different levels. I will describe three—the wisdom of classic feminine patterns of organization, the wisdom of feminine creativity, and feminine wisdom itself.

Most businesses are organized according to the standard male organizational principle, which little boys learn while they are still in elementary school. Every time we went to recess, we learned it. For instance, go with me down to a baseball diamond any fine spring day and look at the two teams and answer some questions, first about the team in the field:

~ What's the typical first baseman like? Tall, good glove, good reach, left-handed.

~ The second baseman? Quick, short, right-handed, not a very good arm.

~ Shortstop? Real good arm, great lateral movement, can go to his left or right; he can move in and out, especially out, probably the best all-around athlete on the team, and always right-handed.

~ Third base? Quick reflexes, great arm, always right-handed.

~ The outfielders? Tend to be bigger, can cover a lot of ground, long, accurate throwing arm, generally best as hitters.

When I do this exercise in corporate settings, those boys—now grown men—are generally tuned in, helping everyone to see the fine art of role differentiation and the detailed division of labor according to height, skill, temperament, and finely articulated skills. Most men can define the positions according to whether left- or right-handed is possible or preferred. But most women—except younger ones who have played baseball and therefore already know this male mode of organization—are not involved and couldn't care less. I push them a bit, ask them why they are not interested, to which they generally respond that this is boring. They become even more bored when we introduce the batting order:

~ Who's the first batter? What is his assignment? Lead off; get on base.

~ Second batter? Move first batter around.

~ Third? First power hitter.

~ Fourth? What is the fourth batter called? Cleanup!
What's his job? Bring everyone home!

At this moment I stop the process, turn to the women and ask, "What do you think of all of this?" Almost always the first answer is something like, "It's silly. It's ridiculous." And almost always the second answer is something like, "I never guessed it was so intricate. And that everybody seems to know the same thing—even used the same phrases—'good glove, great arm, lead-off batter, cleanup hitter, bring 'em home.'"

Carol Gilligan, in her book *In a Different Voice*, notes that these assumptions have been operative for a long time:

> From the games they play, boys learn both the independence and the organizational skills necessary for coordinating the activities of large and diverse groups of people. By participating in controlled and socially approved competitive situations, they learn to deal with competition in a relatively forthright manner—to play with their enemies and compete with their friends—all in accordance with the rules of the game. . . . The assumption, then, is that the male model is the better one since it fits the requirements for modern corporate success. . . . Given the realities of adult life, if a girl does not want to be left dependent on men, she will have to learn to play like a boy.[15]

Many girls, of course, have learned to play like boys. The problem is that most boys never do learn to play like girls. Take a second look at an elementary-school playground, this time to watch girls at recess. Some are just talking. Others are playing hopscotch. Still others are jumping rope. Focus on the jump-rope group. On one end of the rope is a girl twirling the rope. On the other end is another girl twirling the rope. And a short line of girls is waiting for their turn to jump rope. They sing a simple little song, swaying back and forth to catch the rhythm so they know when to jump in.

Ask them just one question, similar perhaps to what we might have asked the boys down there on their field of dreams. "Tell me, if the girl on one end is real good at twirling the rope and the girl on the other end is not real good, . . ." One will get just about that far, and the girls will look up in dismay and say, "Mister, it doesn't work that way. We are connected so we have to adjust to one another. You just feel it. You feel the other through the rope and stay together." We might ask, "What do you mean—you just feel the other through the rope?" "It's intuition—it's a rhythm that you feel inside you."

The world of work is changing at breakneck speed from men's ways of structuring to women's ways. We can no longer hope to have a job description for the second baseman that delineates how his work is different from the first baseman's, or when he is expected to back him up or cover first for him. We need to learn to communicate in such a way that we just feel what the other needs. We need to find one another's natural rhythms within our work teams.

No senior manager can effectively continue to give orders from on high and imagine that they will be implemented, which means that we need to learn new patterns of communication and power-sharing. We need to rediscover another aspect of feminine wisdom—feminine creativity. The two creation stories in Genesis demonstrate that difference between the male and female patterns of creativity. The more familiar is found in the first chapter. "In the beginning God created the heavens and the earth. The earth was without form and void, and darkness was upon the face of the deep; and the Spirit [wind, breath] of God was moving over the face of the waters. And God said, 'Let there be light,' and there was light" (Genesis 1:1–3).

Organizations, certainly since the time of the Industrial Revolution, have functioned according to this understanding of authority. It's as if we work in pyramids. At the top is the chief executive officer, who has the best perspective because of his vantage point and, therefore, has the responsibility to make decisions and give orders, which are communicated down the chain of command until the order is eventually implemented. "Let there be light," he says from the heavens, and way down on earth there is light.

When the story of creation à la the male model is fully told in chapter one, another story is told, or at least begun. You'll find it in the second chapter of Genesis. "In the day that the Lord God made the earth and the heavens, when no plant of the field was yet in the earth and no herb of the field had yet sprung up—for the Lord God had not caused it to rain upon the earth, and there was no man to till the ground; but a mist went up from the earth and watered the whole face of the ground" (Genesis 2:4–7).

That's where the story ends. Barely does it begin before it is cut off. But we still get the point. There is more than one way to be creative. This is the feminine way. The earth (Mother Earth, Gaia) causes a mist to rise up, which creates an environment that gives birth to life. The potential was always present, but the mist has to create the conditions so that the potential can be brought to full flower.

There is much talk in the business world about *empowerment*. It is very hard to "implement policies of empowerment" if we stay stuck in the male mode of creativity. A memo announcing that we will now share power so that everyone can be more creative and fulfilled at work will not do it. Better to create a safe environment where each person's potential can be realized.

There is still a third level at which we can experience Sophia, the embodiment of feminine wisdom. She not only teaches us another system of organization (the jump rope versus the baseball team); she not only teaches us another way to bring life to its full potential (the mist that creates a life-giving environment versus the commands from on high); but she gives us a radical reorientation to life itself.

The figure who most fully personifies this perspective for me is a woman named Shug (as in Sugar) from Alice Walker's *The Color Purple*. Listen to this description of her from Celie, a young woman who has just fallen in love with Shug:

> Shug a beautiful something, let me tell you. She frown a little, look out cross the yard, lean back in her chair, look like a big rose.
>
> She say, My first step from the old white man was trees. Then air. Then birds. Then other people. But one day when I was sitting quiet and feeling like a motherless

child, which I was, it come to me: that feeling of being part of everything, not separate at all. I knew that if I cut a tree, my arm would bleed. And I laughed and I cried and I run all around the house. I knew just what it was. In fact, when it happen, you can't miss it.[16]

Celie reflects on this and realizes that she has a certain notion of God that limits her capacity to open up to the wonders of creation, even her own creation:

Well, us talk and talk bout God, but I'm still adrift. Trying to chase that old white man out of my head. I been so busy thinking bout him I never truly notice nothing God make. Not a blade of corn (how it do that?) not the color purple (where it come from?). Not the little wild-flowers. Nothing.

Now that my eyes opening, I feels like a fool.[17]

For some time women theologians have been talking about the need to get beyond the patriarchal God. Men at midlife need this just as much as those women theologians. The great task for the rest of our lives—the dialogue with the self—will have much more vitality if we can "chase that old white man out of our head" and welcome Sophia into our souls.

THE RITE OF ENCOUNTERING THE SOUL MATE

We must acknowledge that most men at midlife are not experiencing the anima development in its final stages, that is, in the encounter with Sophia, feminine wisdom. Rather, in midlife most men are caught on a snag as the soul mate transforms herself from Eve to Helen. Fortunately the Hebrew Scriptures tell us of a man who is caught on this same snag. His name is David, and he is our traveling companion for this part of our journey.

Many men will know of this soul brother and his one fateful day (2 Samuel 11:1–27). It happened that, late one afternoon, when David arose from his couch and was walking upon the roof of the king's house, he saw a woman bathing, and the woman was very beautiful. And David sent and inquired about the woman. And one said, "Is not this Bathsheba, the daughter of Eliam, the wife of Uriah the Hittite?" So David sent messengers, and took her; and she came to him, and David lay with her. Then she returned to her house. And the woman conceived; and she sent and told David, "I am with child" (11:2–5).

What a helluva thing! Here he is. David. The great King of Israel. The one from whose progeny the Messiah will come. And here the Bible announces to the entire world that David went middle-aged crazy and used his power to seduce his Helen. The man is a disgrace to humanity, and at the same time he is the epitome of manhood. Plumb *that* mystery! As you plumb it, read the whole story of David: the victory over Goliath (1 Samuel 17:1–58); that beautiful love relationship with Jonathan (1 Samuel 18:1–4); and the confusing and troubling relationship with Saul (e.g., 1 Samuel 18–19; 23:14–24:22; 26:1–25); the military victories with all their brutality; the harp and the poetry. And make sure you follow him all the way to the end. The weakness. The impotence. The one last futile attempt to get it up with Abishai:

> Now King David was old and advanced in years; and although they covered him with clothes, he could not get warm. "Therefore," his servants said to him, "Let a young maiden be sought for my lord the king, and let her wait upon the king, and be his nurse; let her lie in your bosom, that my lord the king may be warm." So they sought for a beautiful maiden throughout all the territory of Israel, and found Abishai the Shunammite, and brought her to the king. The maiden was very beautiful; and she became the king's nurse and ministered to him; but the king knew her not. (1 Kings 1:1–4)

When you have read the whole story, from glorious beginning to final frustration, return to that warm spring afternoon when David plucked Bathsheba from the flock. And start asking questions. *What* happened? How can any sane man merely see a woman, even a beautiful woman, even a beautiful woman who is bathing (we assume naked or near naked . . . right?) on her roof so the king could see? How could any sane man just see a woman and fall in love so suddenly, so totally, so desperately?

What was Bathsheba doing on that roof? In the middle of the afternoon? Naked? And then, how did David get that power just to demand that she come to him and lie with him? Is that only for kings and presidents? Or do the rest of us have that power, too?

And, oh my God, she's pregnant. What does he do? He schemes, of course. He tries to work something out. And he does in Uriah. He has Bathsheba's husband killed. Now stop. And ask, Who is this man David? How can we learn from his experience so that when we are old and worn out and can't get warm, we won't still believe we need a beautiful young woman to nurse us? How can we find that nurturing feminine within us? How can our encounter with the soul mate be shaped so that we can grow beyond that fateful day when we spied our Bathsheba?

These are important questions. They are particularly problematic for us as we dare to create a mystery rite that will help us deal with the midlife encounter with the anima, which generally involves the transition from Eve to Helen, even as we realize that a lifelong encounter with the anima should eventually address other transitions as they become appropriate during the second half of life.

To help us in this process we invite another woman to escort us through the midlife passage and guide us toward more mature issues. She is the Woman with the Ointment who bathed Christ's feet with her tears and dried them with her hair. She is such a mysterious figure that we cannot hope to meet her unless we cross the threshold into her sacred space. This rite might be called a guided fantasy. We call it The Anointing.

Begin with preparation. This time it is crucial to read the text:

> One of the Pharisees asked him to eat with him, and he went into the Pharisee's house, and sat at table. And behold, a woman of the city, who was a sinner, when she learned that he was sitting at table in the Pharisee's house, brought an alabaster flask of ointment, and standing behind him at his feet, weeping, she began to wet his feet with her tears, and wiped them with the hair of her head, and kissed his feet, and anointed them with ointment. (Luke 7:36–38)

Make sure you know who those Pharisees are. They are the people who believed in the resurrection; the wealthy, more politically conservative Sadducees did not. The Pharisees supported stable government; the Essenes wanted to withdraw from political life. In short, the Pharisees were good, middle-class folks who went to work, paid their taxes, complained about freeloaders, and believed in law and order. They are all around us still. Indeed, they are well established within us. They control most of us.

Also make sure you know who this woman is. She is not a saint. Indeed, she is a Helen for hire—a sinner. All she has are tears, natty hair, and some ointment. Actually it's perfumed oil: sweet, sensuous, expensive, the stuff that makes a person the Anointed One. (*Messiah* is the Hebrew word for "anointed one"; *Christ* is the Greek word. Jung's word is *Self.*)

Now we are prepared to cross the threshold for our own anointing. The place belongs to the Pharisees (think "the good, middle-class, law-abiding folk"). Every place of anointing originally belongs to such folk. Listen to them recite the codes you have been hearing since you were a little boy. "Don't play with yourself. It's dirty." "If I catch you masturbating, then . . ." "You know you can go blind, or lose the gray matter, or your hair will fall out later." "You're just like your father." "You men are so helpless." "Sex is a sacred thing to be practiced infrequently." "Keep it in your knickers."

As the litany of laws drones on, notice the woman. Notice her hair. The shape of her body. Her feet. Her eyes. Her tears. Her person. Her depth. Her love. And let her open her alabaster flask of ointment, and slowly kneel at your feet, her hair falling down, her tears flowing freely, her ointment pouring out ready to make you a self. (Pause.)

As she begins to anoint you ask her to tell you about herself, her womanly feminine self. Ask her all the questions you ever wanted to know but were afraid to ask. Ask her. And listen deeply. Very deeply. (Pause.) It could be wise to write down what she has to tell you. Eventually you are going to have to leave this place, and you may want to remember her wisdom. (Pause.)

When the time comes and you must leave, be warned that as you leave, the lawful good folk will needle and chide you. Try to keep yourself centered—it's hard—as you talk to them about sin and forgiveness. But do not judge these people of the code. Remember, "Judge not that you be not judged." The people of the code you need to fear are not outside you. That would be projection. The really fearsome ones are deep within you and me. (Pause.)

Before you step back across the threshold, thank the woman and bid her to go in peace. Now rest.

6

THE DIALOGUE WITH THE SELF

When men arrive at the soul's river, they are entrapped by their personae. They come with some vague sense that the first part of their life is over and they need to find "the program for the second half of life." So they start the crossing.

But the fact is that many men never make it across the river. They begin by stripping off all the burdens they have accepted as they constructed their identities. Then they swim out into the unknown to discover the bad stuff of the shadow that they have projected onto others and to experience the animating new life that accompanies the encounter with the soul mate. But they still fail to get all the way to the other side. Suddenly, they panic and find themselves beating a hasty retreat back to the safe familiarity of the persona, becoming "conspicuously virtuous" and "zealously monogamous," actually slipping back into the old pattern of making names for themselves again.

Crossing the soul's river must be seen for what it is—"a prolonged psychological journey." It must also be seen for what it can do—lead to an ongoing dialogue with the self. If men do not understand the purpose of the crossing, they will not survive its trials. "What one can gain from going all the way through the midlife transition, then, is a sense of an internal non-egoistic self and the feeling of integrity and wholeness that results from living in conscious contact with it." The self "would become the foundation for a new experience and integrity, based on an internal center."[1]

The crucial shift in midlife is the change in consciousness from a persona-orientation to a self-orientation. The persona can be pictured as a box, which represents Daniel Levinson's "individual life structure," or Erik Erikson's "identity," or Carl Jung's "persona." Its hard outer edges help to define one's personality. Starting in the lower corner in youth, the box is rather undefined. But as one goes through adulthood—building toward the upper right side—the box becomes restrictive until it pinches, cracks, and, for many men, breaks down. Although this is not easy to endure, it is good because men can head out toward the unknown and seek for something quite different.

At the center of this new dynamism is a core, a nucleus, a heart that keeps this circle either from spinning out of control or losing the integrity of its shape. This center is the self. And the line that runs between the box and the found center is the midlife passage. The journey's goal is to establish a dialogue with the self. This is the real payoff for all the pain and confusion of midlife.[2]

WHAT IS THE SELF?

I find it helpful to draw on a number of ancient and modern sources to guide us to a deeper understanding. In the Gospel of Thomas, a Gnostic gospel dating from early in the Christian era, Jesus of Nazareth expresses the idea without actually using the word *self*: "If you bring forth what is within you, what you bring forth will save you. If you do not bring forth what is within you, what you do not bring forth will destroy you."[3] The Synoptic Gospels all quote Jesus as saying essentially the same thing: "Whoever would save his life will lose it, and whoever loses his life for my sake will find it" (Matthew 16:25). "Whoever seeks to gain his life will lose it, but whoever loses his life will preserve it" (Luke 17:33).

Meister Eckhart, a thirteenth-century Christian mystic theologian, expressed the idea more forcefully: "To get to the core of God at his greatest, one must get to the core of himself at his least, for no one can know God who has not first known himself. Go to the depths of the soul, the secret place of the Most High, to the roots, to the heights; for all that God can do is focused there."[4]

C. G. Jung, as discussed earlier, had a terrifying experience at midlife that allowed the self to express itself in such a way that its nature could be explored. He discovered a force that he termed "a universal will that might be purposive."[5]

As a young man my goal had been to accomplish something in my science. But then, I hit upon a stream of lava, and the heat of its fires reshaped my life. That was the primal stuff which compelled me to work upon it, and my works are a more or less successful endeavor to incorporate this incandescent matter into the contemporary picture of the world.[6]

As early as 1921 Jung was writing about the relationship between the ego, which he described as the center of consciousness, and the self, the corresponding center of the unconscious, indeed of the whole being.

By ego I understand a complex of representations which constitutes the center of my field of consciousness and appears to possess a very high degree of continuity and identity. . . . But, inasmuch as the ego is only the center of my field of consciousness, it is not identical with the totality of the psyche. . . . Hence I discriminate between the ego and the self, since the ego is only the subject of my consciousness, while the self is the subject of my totality: hence it also includes the unconscious psyche. In this sense the self would be an (ideal) factor which embraces and includes the ego.[7]

Once he began to see the outlines of the self, Jung continued his quest to know its essence more fully. "My whole being was seeking for something still unknown which might confer meaning on the banality of my life."[8] And he was ready to pay dearly for this discovery.

From the beginning I had conceived my voluntary confrontation with the unconscious as a scientific experiment which I myself was conducting and in whose outcome I was vitally interested. Today I might equally well say that it was an experiment which was being conducted on me. . . . I stood helpless before an alien world. I was living in a constant state of tension. . . . My enduring these storms was a question of brute strength.

But there was a demonic strength in me, and from the beginning there was no doubt in my mind that I must find the meaning of what I was experiencing in these fantasies. When I endured these assaults of the unconscious I had an unswerving conviction that I was obeying a higher will and that feeling continued to uphold me until I had mastered the task.[9]

Jung's account of his quest for the self should alert us to some of the inevitable challenges. The quest requires a high tolerance for ambiguity. And it takes a great deal of energy.

Heinz Kohut, a Freudian writer, in his book *The Restoration of the Self*, comments on the strain of living with that ambiguity.

My investigation contains hundreds of pages dealing with the psychology of the self—yet it never assigns an inflexible meaning to the term self, and it never explains how the essence of the self should be defined. But I admit this fact without contrition or shame. We cannot, by introspection and empathy, penetrate to the self, *per se;* only its introspectively or emphatically perceived psychological manifestations are open to us.[10]

Edwin Edinger, a Jungian analyst, struggles with this ambiguity in his book *Encounter with the Self*.

The term 'self' is used by Jung to designate the transpersonal center and totality of the psyche. It constitutes the greater, objective personality, whereas the ego is the lesser, subjective personality. Empirically the self cannot be distinguished from the God-image.

There is in the unconscious a transpersonal center of latent consciousness and obscure intentionality. The discovery of the center, which Jung called the self, is like the discovery of extraterrestrial intelligence. Man is now no longer alone in the psyche and in the cosmos. The vicissitudes of life take on new and enlarged meaning. Dreams, fantasies, illness, accident and coincidence become potential messages from the unseen Partner with whom we share our life.

At first, the encounter with the Self is indeed a defeat for the ego: but with perseverance . . . light is born
from the darkness. One meets the "Immortal One" who
wounds and heals, who casts down and raises up, who
makes small and makes large—in a word, the One who
makes one Whole.[11]

Robert Bly writes about our responsibility to these forces that
constitute the self, giving us some hint of the significant role we
play. "Our work then as men and women is not only to free ourselves from family cages and collective mind sets, but to release
transcendent beings from imprisonment and trance."[12] Incredible,
isn't it? *Our* task is to release the transcendent beings from imprisonment and trance. Their liberation, somehow, depends on *our*
courage and *our* consciousness.

David Whyte helps us to see how a new and mature relationship with the self is very different from simple self-centeredness or
self-aggrandizement. He wrote a poem called "Self Portrait." He
had been to the van Gogh exhibit in Amsterdam, where he saw a
whole section of self-portraits. If this feat of self-presentation could
be accomplished with painting, then perhaps one can also do it
with words. So he took a piece of paper and wrote the words *Self
Portrait* at the top of the page. He imagined he would say something
about his jawline or his cheekbone, but instead he wrote:

It doesn't interest me if there is one God
or many gods.
I want to know if you belong or feel
abandoned.
If you know despair or can see it in others.
I want to know
if you are prepared to live in the world
with its harsh need
to change you. If you can look back
with firm eyes
saying this is where I stand. I want to know
if you know
how to melt into that fierce heat of living
falling toward

the center of your longing. I want to know
if you are willing
to live, day by day, with the consequence of love
and the bitter
unwanted passion of your sure defeat.

I have been told, in *that* fierce embrace, even
the gods speak of God.[13]

Who do we see in our mirror? Do we have the courage to examine ourselves with our own questions and our own untapped capacities, to probe deeply enough at our reflection so that we see not some mere reflection of the persona we have cultivated in the first half of life, but our own self peering back at us? What a challenge to look *behind* the mask, to greet the true self underneath it all!

NARCISSISM AND MEN

Many are afraid to look at themselves, not only because they are afraid of what they might find, but also because our culture tells us that to focus on oneself in such a way is downright narcissistic—a psychological version of masturbation. Although narcissism can be seen by classical psychotherapy in neutral terms as "simple self-regard," many tend to see it in negative terms. Here is one such assessment:

> "Narcissism (of the unhealthy type) is a *self-centeredness* or an apparent high regard for oneself utilized as a defense against underlying unpleasant linkages" [to quote S. E. Pulver, writing in the *Journal of the American Psychoanalytic Association*]. This condition is based on the overcompensation of inferiority complexes and the accompanying fear of self-depreciated life situations. This may also be accompanied by the so–called "narcissistic vulnerability," a tendency to register with oversensitive antennae the least sign of challenge to one's self-esteem and to react with distress. [This manifests itself] with oscillations "from one extreme to the other," from feelings of grandiosity to those of absolute worthlessness.[14]

This clinical diagnosis was applied to me by a specialist who offered to restructure the complexes or objects over years of therapy.

When I met with my own therapist (after he returned from hiking in the Swiss Alps), he cast things in a different light: "Of course you're narcissistic. That's not the issue. The issue is not whether you are this or that diagnosis. The issue is what you do with your self-knowledge. The issue is transformation." This same question applies to each man. What do you do with this self-knowledge? What can you learn about your transformation?

Narcissism is an important issue not just for me but for all of us. Christopher Lasch's 1979 book *The Culture of Narcissism* discerned, "Strategies of narcissistic survival now present themselves as emancipation from the repressive conditions of the past, thus giving rise to a 'cultural revolution' that reproduces the worst features of the collapsing civilization it claims to criticize."[15] Lasch argues that the economic person has given way to the psychological person, that the narcissistic individual is characterized by his or her untrammeled striving for happiness and ego pleasure, and that the narcissistic person has become the dominant type of mass man since the 1970s.

For most of the twentieth century, certainly since the writings of Freud on this subject, the operative myth for men has been the myth of Oedipus, who is forewarned that he will kill his father and marry his mother, and then fulfills that fate. Lasch rightly insists that since the 1970s the myth of Narcissus has become the primary myth with which men need to contend. No longer do we have distant and threatening fathers whom we wish to kill so that we can fully love and be loved by our mothers. Now we are perplexed by different questions. "Who am I really? Is there more to me than the image I have created? Is there something beneath the surface?" Moreover, we are haunted by female figures to whom (in too many cases) we assign secondary roles in our cosmic dramas. Unfortunately, these roles are only bit parts, mere echoes of the inflated aims of our egos.

The ancient myth of Narcissus speaks to these issues. The story has been rendered in many ways, but Ovid's description remains the classic. We are told that

> [by the time Narcissus] reached his sixteenth year and
> might seem either boy or man, many youths and many

maidens sought his love; but in that slender form was pride so cold that no youth, no maiden touched his heart. Once as he was driving the frightened deer into his nets, a certain nymph of strange speech beheld him, resounding Echo, who could neither hold her peace when others spoke, nor yet begin to speak till others had addressed her. . . . When she saw Narcissus wandering through the fields, she was enflamed with love and followed him by stealth.[16]

Sensing that someone was there, Narcissus called out, "Is anyone here?" "Here," Echo echoed. "Come," he cried. "Come," she repeated his every word. "Let us meet," he begged. "Let us meet," she answered as she rushed to him, ready to throw her arms around his neck. But young Narcissus was not able to love her, for he loved to hear his own voice and was incapable of listening to another. Spurned, lovely Echo fled through the woods to a cave in the hills, where she pined until all her flesh was gone, leaving only bones— and a voice. Eventually even the bones turned to stone, and only her voice was left, an echo which we can still hear today.

Meanwhile, Narcissus laid down in a pasture and saw his own image in a pond. Dazed by his own beauty, he burned with love for himself and pondered, "What shall I do?" Shamed by his love for himself, he yearned to die. But even in death, he continued to gaze at his own reflection in the Stygian pool. And as they prepared for the funeral, they could not find his body, but in its place they found a flower with white petals encircling the yellow center.

What a tragic tale. A wise professor once said about the Hebrew prophets, "They didn't proclaim those dire prophecies so they would come true. They prophesied so that those who heard could amend their ways, change their lives, and avoid the very fate the prophets proclaimed so powerfully." I believe the same must be true of those Greek myths. They were told so we could learn from our character disorders and invite personal transformation to follow from those learnings.

Two learnings from this are transformational. First, many a midlife male looks for a woman like Echo. We are too often tired of our wives, who seem frumpy in their familiarity (even though other men might find them attractive), and we yearn for a beautiful young woman (our personal Helen) who will be willing to listen to our every thought, smile with approval, and respond to us with adoration—an Echo would do nicely. And the likelihood is that this yearning can be fulfilled. Lots of younger women seem to be at hand—with the bodies of 16-year-olds or 26-year-olds or even 36-year-olds and the appropriate depth and maturity. When we talk to them, they can mindlessly echo back whatever platitude just came out of our mouth.

In this arrangement we hear nothing of real value about our life or ourself. Mario Jacoby notes that the unfolding of the self can occur only within a supportive context: "The energy underlying the process of individuation, and this process—stimulated and directed by the self—remains dependent on a facilitating environment. It needs 'significant others' in order to unfold."[17] Men who live superficial lives seek superficial affirmation. We surround ourselves with others who are not invited to be significant, not allowed to challenge us. And this gets worse as we get older. We yearn for pretty, nubile, mindless Echo, a yes-woman who will delight with us as we stare at our reflection in the still water.

We need to have the courage to invite these significant others to disturb our pools of water, trouble our images, move through the infatuation with our masks, take us beneath the surface to where we might find our deeper selves:

THE WELL OF GRIEF

Those who will not slip beneath
    the still surface of the well of grief

turning downward through its black water
to the place we cannot breathe

will never know the source from which we drink,
    the secret water, cold and clear,

nor find in the darkness glimmering
the small, round coins
thrown by those who wished for something else.[18]

It is only when we go beneath the surface that we can hope to dialogue with the self and thereby get on with the program for the second half of life. Once the dialogue is begun, remarkable things can happen. Indeed, the self will finally be freed from the trance that has kept it in silence, and it will eventually answer. And the answer will give your life new meaning and the will to fulfill it.

Dag Hammarskjöld, the former secretary general of the United Nations, seemed to carry the weight of the whole world on his shoulders. He writes in his diary (published as *Markings*) about his dialogue with the self:

> I don't know Who—or what—put the question. I don't know when it was put. I don't even remember answering. But at some moment I did answer yes to Someone— or Something—and from that hour I was certain that existence is meaningful and that, therefore, my life, in self-surrender, had a goal. From that moment I have known what it means "not to look back" and "to take no thought for the morrow."[19]

Victor Frankl had a similar experience. At one point he was in a Nazi concentration camp enduring trials that were as bad as the trials of legendary Job. In the depths of his deepest despair, he struggled to continue his dialogue with the self (from which he later created logotherapy). He thought he heard an answer. That answer gave his life meaning—and the meaning gave him the will to live:

> We were at work in a trench. The dawn was gray around us; gray was the sky above; gray the snow in the pale light of dawn; gray the rags in which my fellow prisoners were clad, and gray their faces. I was struggling to find the *reason* for my sufferings, my slow dying. In a last violent protest against the hopelessness of imminent death, I sensed my spirit piercing through the enveloping gloom. I felt it transcend that hopeless, meaningless world, and from somewhere I heard a victorious "Yes" in answer to my question of the existence of an ultimate purpose. At that moment a light was lit in a distant farmhouse, which stood on the horizon as if painted there, in the midst of the miserable gray of a dawning morning in Bavaria. "Et lux in tenebris lucet"—and light shineth in the darkness.[20]

Both of these men recorded their struggle to find meaning and their victories, but I believe the greatest record is to be found in the book of Job, which was written 25 centuries ago.

JOB AS OUR SOUL BROTHER

This final soul task is different from the first three—not only in its depth and significance but also in its unfamiliarity. This task requires us to pace and explain ourselves more carefully and fully. It also requires us to raise questions we cannot hope to answer, at least not at this stage in our lives. We have to live questions in such a way that the questions become so lively that we become slightly crazy. We need to lose the safe confines of our own identity and of our own time, and merge with Job by entering the eternal now, the worship present.

Job is such an enigmatic figure it would help to have some additional interpreters. Fortunately, we have two fine ones. C. G. Jung wrote a book entitled *Answer to Job* as he was pulling himself through the last stages of his midlife crisis.[21] The other interpreter is William Blake, who in 1825, at the age of 65, created *Illustrations on the Book of Job,* better known as "Blake's Inventions."[22] This was his last major completed work, his masterpiece—a book of pictures, half of which are included with this volume.

The First Invention features Job, his family, and his sheep. This is Job's persona, nearly asleep inside. He has created a wonderful individual life structure, an admirable identity:

> There was a man in the land of Uz, whose name was Job; and that man was blameless and upright, one who feared God and turned away from evil. There were born to him seven sons and three daughters. He had seven thousand sheep, three thousand camels, five hundred yoke of oxen, and five hundred she-asses, and very many fine servants; so that this man was the greatest of all the people of the east. (Job 1:1–3)

You would have thought that such a righteous man would be content to live out his days to the end, which seems near. Maybe it's the setting sun and the rising moon—a new moon. Or maybe

Blake's First Invention

it's that all the musical instruments are hanging on the tree, none making a joyful sound. Or maybe it's just that all his possessions, all those sheep, are lined up in rows, row after boring row. Maybe it's just the look on Job's face. Blake seems to look right through the persona, right through the righteous mask, right through all those signs of success, right through the surface into Job's depths. Here in the depths, Blake finds emptiness.

Yet something seems to be underway deep within Job, something that is uncomfortable. Job is now aware that beneath the facade is much more. In the Second Invention, his wife still has her book open on her lap, just as they both did in the first picture. What is that book anyway? The Good Book? The accountant's profit-and-loss statement for all those sheep? The annual report from the re-

Blake's Second Invention

tirement fund? Whatever, Job has closed his book. His face is coming alive. Surely his eyes are beginning to search and his ears are perking up and his heart is beating a little faster. He senses danger.

Job cannot even imagine that there might be some opportunity getting ready to knock; he sees only the danger. What is hidden from him is the great cosmic drama that is starting to unfold out in some other sphere, like that primordial time. The central figure in this drama, at this moment, is God. But I need your help on this. Look at that figure at the top, the one in the halo. Is that God? It also looks a lot like Job. Notice that God has the book open just as Job did in the first picture. But maybe God is supposed to look like Job (wasn't Adam created in God's image?). Well, they have the same eyes, same robe, same beard, same book, practically the same everything.

No, they have different hair. God has spiked hair. That bothers me. I hope it bothers you, too. God is not supposed to have spiked hair! I'm sure that it says that somewhere in the Bible. This causes me to wonder about the artist, about this man William Blake. Was he sane? A lot of other people have wondered about this, too. In fact so many wondered about Blake's sanity that William Wordsworth had to defend him. "There are some who think this man is mad, but I prefer the madness of this man to the sanity of others."[23] We will take Wordsworth at his word, but let us not forget that we may be dealing with a madman here.

Next notice that muscular youth streaking across the center of the page showing off his speed and power. His real name is *Satan*, which is Hebrew for "adversary." Here are the great primordial adversaries, God and Satan, Good and Evil. But the contrast between them seems like bad news. God looks old and tired; Satan looks great, a hunk, a powerful, dynamic, attractive, stunning hunk of a man, of a *young* man.

Blake tells us elsewhere that we *need* these adversaries:

Without Contraries is no progression. Attraction and Repulsion, Reason and Energy, Love and Hate, are necessary to Human existence. From these contraries spring what the religious call Good and Evil. Good is the passive that obeys Reason. Evil is the active springing from Energy. Good is heaven. Evil is hell.[24]

How easy this seems for Blake to say. He's sixty-five, probably well beyond his midlife crisis. But we're just into ours. And Job, why he's barely begun.

In the Third Invention (not pictured here), all hell breaks loose for the first time. Neither Job nor God is in the picture. Satan, that demonic force, is loose in the land, killing off Job's children and thereby inducing the breakdown of Job's persona.

The Fourth Invention tells of those messengers who come to inform Job that everything he has worked for in the first half of his life is being destroyed. Piece by piece the persona is cracking, the life structure is crumbling. Each messenger brings another broken piece:

~ "The oxen were plowing and the donkeys were feeding beside them, and the Sabeans fell on them and carried them off, and killed the servants with the edge of the sword; I alone have escaped to tell you."

~ "The fire of God fell from heaven and burned up the sheep and the servants, and consumed them; I alone have escaped to tell you."

~ "The Chaldeans formed three columns, made a raid on the camels and carried them off, and killed the servants with the edge of the sword; I alone have escaped to tell you."

~ "Your sons and daughters were eating and drinking wine in their eldest brother's house, and suddenly a great wind came across the desert, struck the four corners of the house, and it fell on the young people, and they are dead; I alone have escaped to tell you." (Job 1:14–19)

Through all of this Job defiantly refuses to give up his righteous identity, even though his church, his sanctuary, has receded into the background and some strange, awesome, primitive Druidic structures have replaced it. But Job will not abandon his good name.

In fact, in the Fifth Invention, Job makes it pretty clear that he is committed to the age-old strategy of midlife men—reconstitute that old persona. He becomes what I call "zealously monogamous." Isn't that sweet the way Mrs. Job hangs on to his arm? Even more, he becomes "conspicuously virtuous." It's as if Job says, "Honey, invite in all the beggars so I can give them some alms." Meanwhile, God looks

Blake's Fourth Invention

real sad and tame. God's spiked hair has been trimmed or combed out. Satan is having a heyday, terrorizing the nice little angels.

In Blake's Sixth Invention, it is made clear that the reconstitution–of–the–persona strategy is not going to work. The figure in the center is Satan. Notice what he has in his right hand. When four arrows are seen, one can know that trouble is coming and that

Did I not weep for him who was in trouble? Was not my Soul afflicted for the Poor

Behold he is in thy hand: but save his Life

5

Then went Satan forth from the presence of the Lord
And it grieved him at his heart
Who maketh his Angels Spirits & his Ministers a Flaming Fire

London. Published as the Act directs March 8. 1825. by W.ᴹ Blake N.ˢ 3 Fountain Court Strand

Proof

Blake's Fifth Invention

everything is about to spin out of control. Now look at what is in the other hand—a jar full of boils. These are smiting Job. The border at the bottom completes this image. Broken are the rod and the staff, which are supposed to comfort us. Smashed is the cup, which is supposed to overflow, maybe even with goodness and mercy. In summary, not a happy picture for Job.

In Blake's Eighth Invention (not shown here), we get a general shot of Job with boils all over his body. Wounds everywhere. (Wounds, *blissere*, bliss.) Job needs to follow his bliss.

No doubt Job does follow his bliss because the next picture is surely the most unbelievable picture of all. Please look at the picture and jot down your questions. Here are my questions: Who's

Blake's Sixth Invention

who here? Is God the one with the halo looking down on the other guy? If so, then who would be Job? Does Job now have spiked hair? Or is God the one in the bed? Is God looking just a bit surprised that any mere mortal, even blameless and upright Job—or, *especially* blameless and upright Job—could ever withstand such a "prolonged psychological journey" as this?

Blake's Ninth Invention

I think the more likely interpretation is that God is the one in bed. God did not think Job could make it this far. I mean, boils are hardly a bliss to follow. So God went to sleep, twenty centuries of stony sleep, vexed to nightmare by a rocking cradle. And now God is suddenly awakened from a deep trance by mere mortal man.

But wait. Look at the border on the bottom. The words might give a clue. "The spirit passed before my face and the hair of my flesh stood up." Ah. So maybe Job is in the bed. And God's still in the halo. With nicely coifed hair. I like that interpretation. It must be right.

But wait again. I now have two rights and no apparent wrongs. This is like when Albert Einstein saw light as both a wave *and* a particle. Einstein focused on the *and*. That's it! That's why this picture is so remarkable. What's important, truly important, is the *and*, the connection, the look from eye to eye, the relationship between Job and God. It's the first stage in the dialogue with the self!

Blake's Tenth Invention (not shown here) depicts Job's three counselors—Eliphaz, Bildad, and Zophar—still trying to get Job to adjust. "Pull up your socks and go home. What's wrong with you?" demands the first. "It must be some type of character disorder. Stay with me for a couple of years, and we'll see if we can help you adjust," offers the second. "Give up, Job," says the third.

In Blake's Eleventh Invention, God is in some exotic embrace with a serpent and has a wild, excessively spiked hairdo. Notice that God also has a cloven foot at the end of the right leg—pointing down to those defeated souls below, who are getting the chains ready for Job's imminent descent. Without a doubt, Job has encountered the shadow.

In Blake's Twelfth Invention (not shown here), the three counselors are joined by a young boy. I find this interesting. All those grown-up counselors have lost their childlike wonder, that's clear. So a fourth counselor, a young boy, joins them.

So often in midlife men find that they need to hear not just from wise counselors, but from a child. The dream that started my own midlife journey comes to mind: I am a young boy walking with an older man to a square of an old Mexican Indian village with a waterfall at the center of the square. After the older man advises me on my journey, he promises what it will be like to com-

Blake's Eleventh Invention

plete it: "If you can get all the way around the square and back to this road, all the energy of the waterfall will be yours."

Blake's Thirteenth Invention portrays the first moment when we hear the Voice speaking from the whirlwind, the waterfall, the whatever. The Voice elevates Job for the dialogue with the self. Jung comments upon this moment:

Blake's Thirteenth Invention

Job is challenged as though he himself were a god. . . .
The conflict becomes acute for Yahweh as a result of a
new factor. . . . The new factor is something that never
occurred before in the history of the world, the un-
heard–of fact that, without knowing it or wanting it, a
mortal man is raised by his moral behavior above the

stars in heaven, from which position of advantage he can behold the back of Yahweh."[25]

Edwin Edinger makes an additional comment on Jung's observation:

> We might ask what does Jung mean by Job's "moral behavior?" I think he refers to Job's refusal to accept responsibility for events that he knows he did not cause. Job's intellectual honesty, his loyalty to his own perception of reality, his integrity in maintaining the distinction between subject and object, between man and God, between finite and infinite—all these go to make up Job's moral behavior, which has forced God to reveal himself.[26]

In short, the midlife passage, so utterly demeaned by our culture, has a moral purpose. In midlife, we can become man enough to gird up our loins and begin the dialogue with God. And the dialogue begins with questions, God's questions:

> Who is this that darkens counsel
> By words without knowledge?
> Gird up your loins like a man,
> I will question you, and you shall declare to me.
> Where were you when I laid the foundation of the earth?
> Tell me, if you have understanding.
> Who determined its measurements?—Surely you know!
> Who stretched the line upon it? (Job 38:1–5)

Wait a minute. There is a certain familiar ring to this questioning. We have heard these words before. But where? It was in the book of Proverbs in a section that describes Sophia, feminine wisdom:

> Ages ago I was set up,
>   at the first, before the beginning of the earth. . . .
> When he marked out the foundations of the earth
>   then I was beside him, like a master workman,
> and I was daily his delight,
>   rejoicing before him always
> rejoicing in his inhabited world
> and delighting in the sons of men. (Proverbs 8:23, 29–30)

We now know, as C. G. Jung knew when he wrote his masterful interpretation of this story, that Job heard Sophia in the voice from the whirlwind.[27] Through the trials and tribulations of midlife he had succeeded in chasing that old–patriarchal–white–man God out of his mind and taking feminine wisdom into his soul. He is *now* ready to live life according to the program for the second half. He is *now* ready for the dialogue with the self. And the dialogue is not going to be a matter of heads talking words at one another. It is going to be a deeply embodied encounter with creation, not unlike, I imagine, my experience, described earlier, when I encountered my Beloved during meditation in a Jesuit monastery.

By the time we have gone all the way around the mandala of midlife, by the time we hear the voice from the whirlwind, we are exhausted. But the energy from the waterfall soon begins to feed us. Our soul will be restored. Our *hywl* will be renewed. And we will begin to see the world, the whole world, in a new light.

On that new day "the morning Stars sang together and all the Sons of God shouted for Joy," says Blake's Fourteenth Invention (not shown here). But that is nothing compared to what happened to the *daughters* of Job. In Blake's Twentieth Invention, we see Job's daughters with their father and his new triptych with a dancing, whirling God right in the center of the center. And this God looks more like Job than ever before. On the border are some wise words. "There were not found Women fair as the Daughters of Job in all the Land and their Father gave them Inheritance among their brethren." The Bible offers more about these daughters. Their names are Turtledove, Cinnamon, and Mascara (as in eye shadow). Biblical translator and scholar Stephen Mitchell says the names symbolize "peace, abundance, and a specifically female kind of grace. The story's center of gravity has shifted from righteousness to beauty, the effortless manifestation of inner peace."[28] How incredible, given that Job's tale was written twenty–five centuries ago, when patriarchy held both women and men in chains. Here patriarchy is turned inside out.

This courageous, highly moral man has survived his "prolonged psychological journey." He has made it all the way round

How precious are thy thoughts
unto me O God
how great is the sum of them

There were not found Women fair as the Daughters of Job
in all the Land & their Father gave them Inheritance
among their Brethren

If I ascend up into Heaven thou art there
If I make my bed in Hell behold Thou
art there

London. Published as the Act directs March 8: 1825 by William Blake N J Fountain Court Strand

Blake's Twentieth Invention

his mandala, *through* his midlife transition. He has made the critical shift from persona-orientation to self-orientation. He can now become his true self—male *and* female did God create them.

Blake's Last Invention offers one final picture. Here is an illustration to love. Job is old now. His daughters and sons *are* beautiful.

Blake's Last Invention

The caption says it all: "After this Job lived an hundred & forty years & saw his Sons & his Sons Sons even four Generations. So Job died being old & full of days."

7

HOPE IN COMMUNITY
AND CONVERSATION

I'm exhausted. Exhausted but exhilarated. For days I have been about the task of writing. Days of solitude. But my time of solitude is about to come to an end, and I will soon return to the drama of everyday life.

The experience is similar to the end of the rite of passage for men at midlife. In this moment I vividly recall driving back to my life after one group's final retreat. We had gone to our deaths, initially by talking about the death's of our fathers and grandfathers, and then by facing our own. We imagined what voices we would be hearing in that moment—our mothers and grandmothers, our partners and friends, our sons and daughters. And we imagined the voices of God and God's partner, Sophia. We provided for one another that facilitating environment so necessary to invite dialogue with the self.

But at a certain point, the retreat had to end. And so it did. And we all got into our cars and headed home. I remember stopping halfway home and just sitting quietly to experience the sadness of the moment.

In a very real sense, this moment at the end of my writing is similarly sad. It's as if this table where I write has become like a sanctuary for me; the place where I pace, like a chapel; the salt marsh that stretches out before my eyes and the woods beyond, like those Elysian Fields and sylvan haunts of primordial time. It's as if all those men who have shared their midlife trials are here with me now. It's as if I am surrounded by a cloud of witnesses. Maybe I should explain.

My little haven is really, some would say, just a lot of books, a couple of tapes, and a computer. The computer is to my left, all its cables, like a life-support system in the intensive care unit, hanging out. In front of me I've set out books. I would guess there are about one hundred books that have become important to me over the years. On my right are files—old sermons, lecture notes from classes, outlines from workshops I've led on worship or the new physics or sexuality or men at midlife. All those files are held in place by my old Bible, the one I used to carry to that reformatory to read those great old stories to those so-called juvenile delinquents. It's now held together with masking tape—for about the last ten years—and some of the pages are about to fall out. But that's all right. In fact, that's great.

Do you remember the Velveteen Rabbit? Once the Rabbit asked the Skin Horse, "What is *real?*" And the Horse answered, "If a child loves you for a long time, . . . then you become *Real*. Generally by the time you are Real, most of your hair is loved off, and your eyes drop out, and you get loose in the joints and very shabby. But these don't matter at all, because once you are Real, you can't be ugly."[1]

My Bible's real. It's lost its luster and can't even hold itself together, but within it, Job is alive—and David and Jacob and Abraham. In it the Woman with the Ointment is teaching men about the mystery of intimacy. And Bathsheba is bathing on her rooftop. And Turtledove (Love Dove), Cinnamon, and Eye Shadow are teaching us all about feminine virtues.

But they are not the only lively ones here. In front of me are not just books, but persons, clustering in little groups to talk with one another about some really great ideas. Over there, for instance, is a group of scientists talking about such wondrous things as dissipative structures and autopoiesis—David Peat, Erich Jantsch, Paul Davies, Gary Zukav, Fritjof Capra, David Bohm, and, of course, Albert Einstein. Important to me is Margaret Wheatley because she can take ideas from one cluster and share them with another. In fact, there she goes now. She's meeting with some business consultants—Peter Block, Bill Bridges, Stephen Covey, Rosabeth Moss Canter, and this modern-day bard, David Whyte, who dares to talk about poetry and the preservation of soul in corporate America, which runs the serious risk of remaining soulless.

Talking about soul causes me to notice another group that is deeply engaged in talking about the soul—Thomas Moore, Rollo May, Paul Tillich, Victor Frankl, and Carl Gustav Jung, who seems to dominate much of the conversation throughout this table. Jung is such a powerful figure that he seems to move all over the place, and as he moves, others follow in his wake—Murray Stein, Edwin Edinger, Mario Jacoby, Daryl Sharp, James Hollis, Nathan Schwartz-Salant, James Hillman, John Sanford, Polly Young-Eisendrath, and gentle Robert Johnson. And listening to them all is John-Raphael Staude, who is gathering anecdotes to write a biography of Jung.

It's fascinating to listen to men and women talk about women and men. Indeed, it is good to see them together. Erik Erikson and Carol Gilligan. Dan Levinson and Gail Sheehy. John Grey and Deborah Tannen. There is also a gathering of men talking about other men, gently talking with one another about the future of gentlemen. Robert Bly, who brings so many other fine thinkers to the table, and Sam Keen, and Aaron Kipnis, and Warren Farrell. And, right next to them, some courageous souls who dare to talk about theology and sexuality—Morton Kelsey and James Nelson, Bob Raines, Roy Oswald, Walter Wink, and June Keener-Wink.

Oh, it's a great group. This is one wonderful get-together at this table. I haven't introduced you to the storytellers—Allan Chinen and Clarissa Pinkola Estés. And I haven't said anything about the novelists and playwrights—Alice Walker, Toni Morrison, James Joyce, or Peter Shaffer. I haven't yet mentioned the poets— W. H. Auden or W. B. Yeats or Derek Walcott or William Blake or David Whyte. But I think I did mention David Whyte. Just a moment ago he was talking to the business consultants. Now he's down here with the poets.

The whole group is beginning to trade places. Mircea Eliade and Desmond Morris are taking the Kwakiutl chief over to talk with someone about transformation masks. Who is that someone? Oh no! Oh yes, it's Jon and Stu, Jon Higgins and Stu Elliot, my dear friends who were hit by speeding cars and killed late one Friday night and early one Saturday morning. They're here, very much here. As are other friends—Steve and Karl, Mark and Brian and Bob, Jim and Sidat. And wonderful wise women.

NOTES

PREFACE

1. William O. Roberts Jr., *Initiation to Adulthood: An Ancient Rite of Passage in Contemporary Form* (New York: The Pilgrim Press, 1982).

2. Hugh Sanborn, ed., *Celebrating Passages in the Church: Reflections and Resources* (St. Louis: Chalice Press, 1998).

3. The Rite of Passage for Men at Midlife was first created for the Asylum Hill Congregational Church in Hartford, Connecticut.

STILL LIVING THE SAME OLD LIFE?

1. See David Whyte, *The Heart Aroused: Poetry and the Preservation of Soul in Corporate America* (New York: Doubleday, 1994); also Peter Block, *Stewardship: Choosing Service over Self-Interest* (San Francisco: Berrett–Koehler Publishers, 1993) and Lee G. Bolman and Terrence E. Deal, *Leading with Soul: An Uncommon Journey of Spirit* (San Francisco: Jossey–Bass Publishers, 1995).

1. TESTING THE DEPTH

1. Erik Erikson, "Youth: Fidelity and Identity," in *Youth: Challenge and Change* (New York: Basic Books, 1963), 11.

2. Erik Erikson, "Eight Ages of Man," in *Childhood and Society* (New York: W. W. Norton and Company, 1950), 261.

3. Ibid., 263.

4. Ibid., 266.

5. Ibid., 268.

6. Daniel Levinson, *Seasons of a Man's Life* (New York: Ballantine Books, 1978), 42.

7. Ibid., 20.

8. See, for example, Allan Chinen, *Beyond the Hero: Classic Stories of Men in Search of Soul* (New York: Jeremy P. Tarcher/Putnam Books, 1993); *In the Ever After: Fairy Tales and the Second Half of Life* (Wilmette, Ill.: Chiron Publications, 1989); and *Once Upon a Midlife: Classic Stories and Mythic Tales to Illuminate the Middle Years* (New York: Jeremy P. Tarcher/Perigee Books, 1992).

9. *The Wisdom of the Dream: Carl Gustav Jung* (Public Media Video, Segaller Films, 1989).

10. Robert Bly, *Iron John: A Book about Men* (New York: Addison–Wesley Publishing, 1990), 68.

11. Rainer Maria Rilke, *Letters to a Young Poet*, trans. M. D. Herter Norton (New York: W. W. Norton, 1934), 34–35.

12. Carl G. Jung, "The Transcendent Function," in *The Structure and Dynamics of the Psyche*, ed. H. Read et al. (Princeton: Princeton University Press, 1972), 396.

13. Albert Einstein, quoted in Margaret Wheatley, *Leadership and the New Science: Learning about Organization from an Orderly Universe* (San Francisco: Berrett-Koehler Publishers, 1993), 5.

14. See John-Raphael Staude, *The Adult Development of C. G. Jung* (Boston: Routledge and Kegan Paul, 1981).

15. Carl Gustav Jung, *Memories, Dreams, and Reflections*, trans. Richard Winston and Clara Winston (New York: Random House, 1961), 177, 179, 192.

16. Donella Meadows, "Whole Earth Models and Systems," *Co-evolution Quarterly* (summer 1982): 23.

17. *The Collected Poems of W. B. Yeats* (New York: Macmillan, 1933), 184–85.

18. Murray Stein, *In Midlife: A Jungian Perspective* (Dallas: Spring Publications, 1983), 26–27.

2. FORGING THE RITE OF PASSAGE FOR MEN

1. Peter Shaffer, *Equus* (New York: Penguin Books, 1973), 82.

2. Ibid., 61–62.

3. Ibid., 82.

4. Ibid., 83.

5. Norman O. Brown, *Love's Body* (New York: Random House, 1966), 15.

6. Joseph Campbell, *Hero with a Thousand Faces* (Princeton: Princeton University Press, 1949), 104.

7. James Hollis, *The Middle Passage: From Misery to Meaning in Midlife* (Toronto: Inner City Books, 1993), 23.

8. Jan O. Stein and Murray Stein, "Psychotherapy, Initiation, and the Midlife Transition," in *Betwixt and Between: Patterns of Masculine and Feminine Initiation*, ed. Louise Carus Mahdi et al. (LaSalle, Ill.: Open Court, 1987), 289.

9. Bly, *Iron John*, 140–41.

10. Daryl Sharp, *The Survival Papers: Anatomy of a Midlife Crisis* (Toronto: Inner City Books, 1988), 31.

11. Robert Johnson, *Innerwork: Using Dreams and Active Imagination* (San Francisco: HarperCollins, 1986), 100.

12. See Mircea Eliade, *Cosmos and History: The Myth of Eternal Return* (New York: Harper Torchbooks, 1954); and *Myth and Reality* (New York: Harper Torchbooks, 1963).

3. THE BREAKDOWN OF THE PERSONA

1. Ronald Grimes, "Masking: Toward a Phenomenology of Exteriorization," *Journal of American Academy of Religion* 63 (September 1975): 510–12.

2. Brown, *Love's Body*, 96–97.

3. Erik Erikson, "The Eight Ages of Man," *Childhood and Society* (New York: W. W. Norton and Company, 1950), 261; and Levinson, *Seasons of a Man's Life*, 42.

4. Lord Byron, "The Prisoner of Chillon," in *Byron: Poetic Works*, ed. Frederick Page (New York: Oxford University Press, 1970), 336.

5. F. David Peat, *Synchronicity: The Bridge between Matter and Mind* (New York: Bantam Books, 1987), 77.

6. Wheatley, *Leadership and the New Science,* 19.

7. Ibid., 19–20.

8. David Whyte, "The Faces at Braga," in *Where Many Rivers Meet* (Langley, Wash.: Many Rivers Press, 1993), 25–27.

9. Erich Jantsch, *The Self-Organizing Universe* (New York: Pergamon Press, 1980), 7.

10. See Chinen, *Beyond the Hero, In the Ever After,* and *Once Upon a Midlife,* as well as Clarissa Pinkola Estés, *Women Who Run with the Wolves: Myths and Stories of the Wild Woman Archetype* (New York: Ballantine Books, 1992). Estés does not write for women alone. Many of her tales, especially "The Skeleton Woman," speak powerfully to men.

11. Aldona Jonaitis, ed., *Chiefly Feasts: The Enduring Kwakiutl Potluck* (New York: American Museum of Natural History, 1991).

4. THE ENCOUNTER WITH THE SHADOW

1. Carl G. Jung, "On the Psychology of the Unconscious" (1917), quoted in *Meeting the Shadow: The Hidden Power of the Dark Side of Human Nature,* ed. Connie Zweig and Jeremiah Abrams (Los Angeles: Jeremy Tarcher, 1991), 3.

2. Robert Bly, "The Long Bag We Drag Behind Us," in *Meeting the Shadow,* ed. Zweig and Abrams, 6–7.

3. Bly, *Iron John,* 206.

4. R. D. Laing, in *Meeting the Shadow,* ed. Zweig and Abrams, xix.

5. John Sanford, *The Invisible Partners: How the Male and Female in Each of Us Affects Relationships* (New York: Paulist Press, 1980), 10.

6. Derek Walcott, "Love after Love," in *The Collected Poems* (New York: Farrar, Straus, and Giroux, 1986), 328.

7. See Conrad W. Weiser, *Healers—Harmed and Harmful* (Minneapolis: Fortress Press, 1994), esp. chapter 5, "Narcissists: Seeking Love, Fearing Closeness." Narcissism is one of three basic defensive styles in response to early wounds that prompt persons to go into the helping professions such as nursing, teaching, or the ministry.

8. Erich Neumann, quoted in *Meeting the Shadow,* ed. Zweig and Abrams, 6.

5. THE ENCOUNTER WITH THE SOUL MATE

1. Sanford, *The Invisible Partners,* 111.

2. Bly, *Iron John,* 135.

3. Gail Sheehy, *Passages: Predictable Crises of Adult Life* (New York: E. P. Dutton, 1974), 144.

4. Sanford, *The Invisible Partners,* 5.

5. Bly, *Iron John,* 124.

6. Robert Johnson, *We: Understanding the Psychology of Romantic Love* (San Francisco: Harper and Row, 1983), 161–62.

7. See Adolf Guggenbuhl-Craig, *Marriage—Dead or Alive* (Zurich: Spring Publications, 1977), 9–10.

8. Sanford, *The Invisible Partners,* 20–21.

9. Hugh of Saint Victor, material given to me by William Welsch, S.J., spiritual director for Ignatian exercises, Jesuit Retreat Center, Wernesville, Pennsylvania.

10. Sharp, *The Survival Papers*, 64–65.

11. This exercise is adapted from Joan B. Bowman and Roy M. Oswald, "Women and Men Together: A Transforming Power for Self, Church, and World" (Washington, D.C.: The Alban Institute, n.d.; unpublished document).

12. Toni Morrison, *Jazz* (New York: Plume Books, 1993), 122–23.

13. Toni Morrison, *Beloved* (New York: Knopf, 1987), 25.

14. Ibid., 21–22.

15. Carol Gilligan, *In a Different Voice: Psychological Theory and Women's Development* (Cambridge: Harvard University Press, 1982), 10–11.

16. Alice Walker, *The Color Purple* (New York: Simon and Schuster, 1982), 202–4.

17. Ibid.

6. THE DIALOGUE WITH THE SELF

1. Stein, *In Midlife*, 26–27.

2. The dialogue with the self is the third of four essential dialogues of life. The first dialogue occurred when we were young. Our primary program was to develop trust, and our primary dialogue was with our parents. If we were successful, then we discovered that we could trust not only our mothers and fathers but the world itself.

The second dialogue is the dialogue with society to establish our identity.

The third dialogue engages the self. If we stay at this task, then we will come to detect the meaning of our own particular life.

The fourth and final dialogue of life transforms the dialogue with the self into a dialogue with the cosmos, with creation itself, and with its creator. See Hollis, *The Middle Passage*, 26–27.

3. Elaine Pagels, *The Gnostic Gospels* (New York: Random House, 1989), 152.

4. Meister Eckhart, source unknown.

5. Staude, *The Adult Development of C. G. Jung*, 27.

6. Jung, *Memories*, 225.

7. Carl Gustav Jung, "Psychological Types" (1921), in *The Basic Writings of C. G. Jung* (New York: Modern Library, 1959), 246–47.

8. Jung, *Memories*, 165.

9. Ibid., 177–78.

10. Heinz Kohut, *The Restoration of the Self* (New York: International Universities Press, 1977), 310–11.

11. Edwin F. Edinger, *Encounter with the Self: A Jungian Commentary on William Blake's Illustrations of the Book of Job* (Toronto: Inner City Books, 1986), 7–9.

12. Bly, *Iron John*, 223.

13. David Whyte, "Self Portrait," in *Fire in the Earth* (Langley, Wash.: Many Rivers Press, 1992), 10.

14. Mario Jacoby, *Individuation and Narcissism: The Psychology of Self in Jung and Kohut*, trans. Myron Gubitz (New York: Routledge, 1991), 83.

15. Christopher Lasch, *The Culture of Narcissism: American Life in an Age of Diminishing Expectations* (New York: W. W. Norton, 1979), xv.

16. This version of Ovid's "Myth of Narcissus" is translated by Louise Vinge and quoted in Nathan Schwartz-Salant, *Narcissism and Character Transformation: The Psychology of Narcissistic Character Disorders* (Toronto: Inner City Books, 1982), 73–76.

17. Jacoby, *Individuation and Narcissism*, 141.

18. David Whyte, "The Well of Grief," in *Where Many Rivers Meet* (Langley, Wash.: Many Rivers Press, 1993), 35.

19. Dag Hammarskjöld, *Markings*, trans. Leif Sjoberg and W. H. Auden (New York: Knopf, 1970), 205.

20. Victor E. Frankl, *Man's Search for Meaning* (New York: Simon and Schuster, 1959), 51–52.

21. Carl Gustav Jung, *Answer to Job*, trans. R. F. Chull (London: Routledge and Kegan Paul, 1954).

22. William Blake, *Illustrations on the Book of Job* (New York: The Pierpont Morgan Library, 1935).

23. Quoted in Hollis, *The Middle Passage*, 36.

24. William Blake, "The Marriage of Heaven and Hell," quoted in Edinger, *Encounter with the Self,* 20.

25. Jung, *Answer to Job*, 29–30.

26. Edinger, *Encounter with the Self,* 50.

27. Jung, *Answer to Job*, 38–41. In identifying Sophia as the one encountered in the whirlwind, Jung writes of her: "This idea of Sophia, or the Sapientia Dei, which is a coeternal and more or less hypostatized pneuma of feminine nature that existed before the Creation . . . [t]his Sophia, who already shares certain essential qualities with the Johannine Logos, is on the one hand closely associated with the Hebrew *Chochma,* but on the other hand goes so far beyond it that one can hardly fail to think of the Indian *Shakti."*

28. Stephen Mitchell, *The Book of Job* (San Francisco: North Point Press, 1987), xxx.

7. HOPE IN COMMUNITY AND CONVERSATION

1. Margery Williams, *The Velveteen Rabbit* (New York: Avon Books, 1975), 13.

FURTHER READING

Auden, W. H. *The Collected Poetry of W. H. Auden*. New York: Random House, 1945.
Blake, William. *Illustrations on the Book of Job*. New York: The Pierpont Morgan Library, 1935.
Block, Peter. *Stewardship: Choosing Service over Self-Interest*. San Francisco: Berrett-Kohler Publishers, 1993.
Bly, Robert. *Iron John: A Book about Men*. New York: Addison–Wesley Publishing, 1990.
Bridges, William. *JobShift: How to Prosper in a Workplace without Jobs*. New York: Addison–Wesley Publishing, 1994.
———. *Managing Transitions: Making the Most of Change*. New York: Addison–Wesley Publishing, 1991.
———. *Transitions: Making Sense of Life's Changes*. New York: Addison–Wesley Publishing, 1980.
Canter, Rosabeth Moss. *Men and Women of the Corporation*. New York: Basic Books, 1977.
Capra, Fritjof. *The Tao of Physics*. Boston: Shambhala, 1991.
———. *The Web of Life*. New York: Anchor Books, 1996.
Chinen, Allan. *Beyond the Hero: Classic Stories of Men in Search of Soul*. New York: Jeremy P. Tarcher/Putnam Books, 1993.
———. *In the Ever After: Fairy Tales and the Second Half of Life*. Wilmette, Ill.: Chiron Publications, 1989.
———. *Once Upon a Midlife: Classic Stories and Mythic Tales to Illuminate the Middle Years*. New York: Jeremy P. Tarcher/Perigee Books, 1992.
Covey, Stephen R. *The Seven Habits of Highly Effective People: Powerful Lessons in Personal Change*. New York: Fireside, 1989.
Edinger, Edward F. *Ego and Archetype*. New York: Penguin Books, 1972.
———. *Encounter with the Self*. Toronto: Inner City Books, 1986.
Estés, Clarissa Pinkola. *Women Who Run with the Wolves: Myths and Stories of the Wild Woman Archetype*. New York: Ballantine Books, 1992.
Farrell, Warren. *Why Men Are the Way They Are*. New York: Berkley Publishing Group, 1988.
Frankl, Victor E. *Man's Search for Meaning*. New York: Simon and Schuster, 1959.
Gilligan, Carol. *In a Different Voice: Psychological Theory and Women's Development*. Cambridge: Harvard University Press, 1982.

Grey, John. *Men Are from Mars, Women Are from Venus.* New York: HarperCollins, 1992.

Hillman, James. *Insearch: Psychology and Religion.* New York: Charles Scribner's Sons, 1967.

———. *The Soul's Code: In Search of Character and Calling.* New York: Random House, 1996.

Hollis, James. *The Middle Passage: From Misery to Meaning in Midlife.* Toronto: Inner City Books, 1993.

Jacoby, Mario. *Individual and Narcissism: The Psychology of Self in Jung and Kohut.* Translated by Myron Gubitz. New York: Routledge, 1991.

Johnson, Robert A. *He: Understanding Masculine Psychology.* New York, Harper and Row Publishers, 1989.

———. *Inner Work: Using Dreams and Active Imagination for Personal Growth.* San Francisco, Harper, 1986.

———. *We: Understanding the Psychology of Romantic Love.* New York, Harper and Row Publishers, 1983.

Jung, C. G. *Answer to Job.* Translated by R. F. Chull. London: Routledge and Kegan Paul, 1952.

———. *Memories, Dreams, Reflections.* Edited by Aniela Jaffe and translated by Richard and Clara Winston. New York: Random House, 1961.

———. *Modern Man in Search of a Soul.* New York: Harcourt, Brace & World, 1933.

———. *The Undiscovered Self.* Translated by R. F. Chull. New York: The New American Library, 1957.

Keen, Sam. *Fire in the Belly: On Being a Man.* New York: Bantam Books, 1991.

Kelsey, Morton, and Barbara Kelsey. *Sacrament of Sexuality: The Spirituality and Psychology of Sex.* Warwick, N.Y.: Amity House, 1986.

Kipnis, Aaron. *Knights without Armor: A Practical Guide for Men in Quest of Masculine Soul.* New York: Jeremy P. Tarcher/Perigee Books, 1991.

Kipnis, Aaron, and Elizabeth Herron. *Gender War: The Quest for Love and Justice between Women and Men.* New York: William Morrow and Company, 1994.

Levinson, Daniel. *Seasons of a Man's Life.* New York: Ballantine Books, 1978.

May, Rollo. *Love and Will.* New York: W. W. Norton and Company, 1969.

———. *Paulus: Reminiscences of a Friendship.* New York: Harper and Row, 1973.

Mitchell, Stephen. *The Book of Job.* San Francisco: North Point Press, 1987.

Moore, Thomas. *Care of the Soul: A Guide for Cultivating Depth and Sacredness in Everyday Life.* New York: HarperCollins, 1992.

———. *Soul Mates: Honoring the Mysteries of Love and Relationship.* New York: HarperCollins, 1994.

Morrison, Toni. *Beloved.* New York: Knopf, 1987.

———. *Jazz.* New York: Plume Books, 1993.

Nelson, James B. *Embodiment: An Approach to Sexuality and Christian Theology.* Minneapolis: Augsburg Publishing House, 1978.

Roberts, William O., Jr. *Initiation to Adulthood: An Ancient Rite of Passage in Contemporary Form.* New York: The Pilgrim Press, 1982.

Sanford, John A. *The Invisible Partners: How the Male and Female in Each of Us Affects Relationships.* New York: Paulist Press, 1980.

———. *The Man Who Wrestled with God.* New York: Paulist Press, 1974.

Schwartz–Salant, Nathan. *Narcissism and Character Transformation: The Psychology of Narcissistic Character Disorders*. Toronto: Inner City Books, 1982.

Shaffer, Peter. *Equus*. New York: Penguin Books, 1973.

Sharp, Daryl. *The Survival Papers: Anatomy of a Midlife Crisis*. Toronto: Inner City Press, 1988.

Sheehy, Gail. *Passages: Predictable Crises of Adult Life*. New York: Addison–Wesley Publishing, 1990.

———. *Understanding Men's Passages: Discovering the New Map of Men's Lives*. New York: Random House, 1998.

Tannen, Deborah. *You Just Don't Understand: Women and Men in Conversation*. New York: Ballantine Books, 1990.

Tillich, Paul. *The Courage to Be*. New Haven: Yale University Press, 1952.

———. *On the Boundary*. New York: Charles Scribner's Sons, 1966.

Walker, Alice. *The Color Purple*. New York: Simon and Schuster, 1982.

Whyte, David. *Fire in the Earth*. Langley, Wash.: Many Rivers Press, 1992.

———. *The Heart Aroused: Poetry and the Preservation of Soul in Corporate America*. New York: Doubleday, 1994.

———. *Where Many Rivers Meet*. Langley, Wash.: Many Rivers Press, 1993.

Wink, Walter. *The Bible in Human Transformation*. Philadelphia: Fortress Press, 1973.

Yeats, W. B. *The Collected Poems of W. B. Yeats*. New York: Macmillan, 1933.

Young–Eisendrath, Polly. *Hags and Heroes: A Feminist Approach to Jungian Psychotherapy with Couples*. Toronto: Inner City Press, 1984.